Scotland's Inland Waterways
Canals, Rivers & Lochs

PJG Ransom

NMS Publishing

Published by NMS Publishing Limited, Royal Museum, Chambers Street, Edinburgh EH1 1JF
© P J G Ransom and NMS Publishing Limited 1999
Series editor Iseabail Macleod

Other titles available in this series	*Fishing & Whaling*	*Sporting Scotland*
	Farming	*Spinning & Weaving*
	Building Railways	*Making Cars*
	Leaving Scotland	*Feeding Scotland*
	Going to School	*Going to Church*
	Scots in Sickness & Health	*Going on Holiday*
	Going to Bed	*Shipbuilding*
	Scottish Bicycles & Tricycles	
Forthcoming titles	*Getting Married*	*Scottish Music Hall, Variety and*
	Scottish Cinema	*Pantomime*
	Engineering	
Other titles by the author include	*Holiday Cruising in Ireland*	*The Archaeology of the Transport*
	Your Book of Canals	*Revolution 1750-1850*
	Waterways Restored	*Scottish Steam Today*
	Loch Earn	*Transport in Scotland through the Ages*
	The Archaeology of Canals	

British Library Cataloguing in Publication Data
A catalogue record of this book is available from the British Library

ISBN 1 901663 22 1

Designed by NMS Publishing Limited
Printed in the United kingdom by Cambridge University Press Printing Division

Acknowledgements
The author is most grateful to the following, who have helped during preparation of this book:
Ms B L Andrian, John Beveridge, Jack Bissett, David Craig, John Crompton, Alec Howie, David E James, Graham Kinder, Keith Kirk, Alistair Lawson, Iain Morrison, James M Stirling.
Thanks too to my agent, Duncan McAra, my editor, Iseabail Macleod, and my wife Elisabeth.

Illustrations: 9, 32, 36, 51, 63, 68, 71, 72: PJG Ransom. 12, 15, 22, 23, 24, 25, 30, 35, 38, 43, 45, 49, 50, 56, 57, 58, 59: National Museums of Scotland. 21, 34, 39, 40, 54, 66: East Dunbartonshire Council. 26: Falkirk Museum Services. 60: British Waterways Authority. 65: John McHale CStJ Maps by PJG Ransom and Elizabeth Robertson.
Illustrations captioned SLA are from the Scottish Life Archive in the National Museums of Scotland.

Cover picture: *Vintage passenger launch* Ratho Princess *cruises along the Edinburgh & Glasgow Union Canal.*

Contents

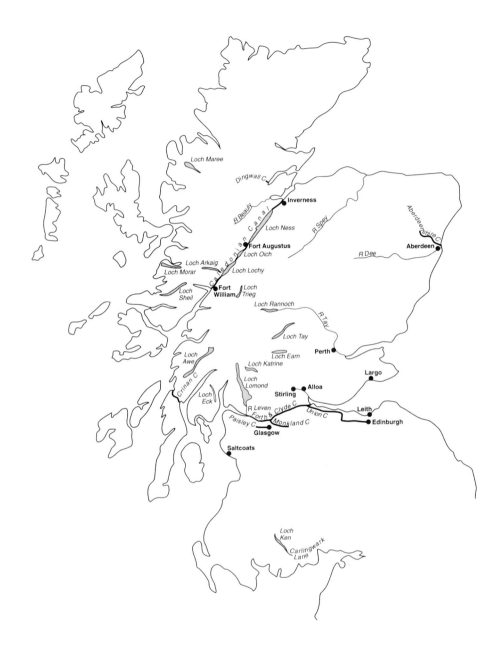

Scotland's inland waterways
(An enlarged map of Central Belt waterways appears on pages 18 and 19)

4

Introduction

'For mere luxury of transportation, such canal-travel stands quite unri-valled.' Thus wrote Sir Archibald Geikie in *Scottish Reminiscences,* published in 1904, of travel on the Edinburgh & Glasgow Union Canal seventy years earlier. He added:

> It was a novel and delightful sensation, which I can still recall, to see fields, trees, cottages, and hamlets flit past, as if they formed a vast moving panorama, while one seemed to be sitting absolutely still...Among its drawbacks, however, are the long detentions at the locks. But as everything was new to me in my first expedition to the west, I remember enjoying these locks with the keenest pleasure, sometimes remaining in the boat, and feeling it slowly floated up or let down, sometimes walking along the margin and watching the rush of water through the gradually opening sluices...the passenger boats on the canal were disused after the opening of the Edinburgh and Glasgow Railway in the spring of 1842.

The period of which he wrote was short-lived and long ago. Yet as I write, in the late 1990s, the most ambitious inland waterway restoration scheme in Britain is under way in Scotland. So, quite independently, is the most ambitious scheme for restoration of an inland waterway vessel. The canals which link Edinburgh and Glasgow, that is to say the Union Canal and the Forth & Clyde Canal, are being restored to navigability, and the paddle steamer *Maid of the Loch* on Loch Lomond is being restored to working order. The canals were closed to navigation in the 1960s; the steamer has lain out of use since 1981.

So this seems a good moment to produce an outline of the history of inland waterways in Scotland, for they form part of the Scottish heritage which has received far less attention than it deserves. This may be because once the closed canals of the Central Belt had been obstructed by unus-able locks and demolished bridges they became purposeless, or at least their purpose was no longer apparent. Yet in their day they were the arteries of transport which made possible the Industrial Revolution, and some were immensely prosperous. The great Burrell shipping family commenced its activities on the canals.

The inland waterways of Scotland have other claims to fame. Much of the earliest development of steamboats took place on Scottish canals, and the first iron boat built in Scotland – the true ancestor of all the great iron and steel ships built on the Clyde – was a canal passenger boat. Scottish canals incorporate structures, such as the staircase locks of the Caledonian Canal and the high aqueducts of the Union Canal, which stand comparison, for grandeur and for the skills of their designers and builders, with any in the British Isles.

There are several respects in which Scottish inland waterways differ from those of England and Ireland. The inland waterways of England comprise, almost entirely, slow-flowing rivers and canals, and most of these link up to form a national system. Those of Ireland are similar, with the important addition of many loughs, some of them very large, into and out of which flow the navigable rivers.

The inland waterways of Scotland, however, comprise firstly the canals: the small canal system of the Central Belt; the Crinan Canal and the Caledonian Canal; and other isolated canals. Secondly, there are many freshwater lochs, some of them very extensive; three are incorporated into the route of the Caledonian Canal but most others are isolated. None the less they have been important as waterways, as routes for transport or travel by water, since the earliest times. Scottish rivers, in their non-tidal lengths, are generally fast-flowing and only a few are or have been navigable for vessels larger than canoes. In this book I have taken inland waterways as ending where the tideway begins – so firths, estuaries and sea lochs are in general outside its scope.

There are two other important features in which Scottish inland waterways contrast with those of England. One is the extent to which they have always been significant for travel by people, as well as for transport of goods. From as early as the eighteenth century, too, some of that travel was recreational, for boats on Highland lochs gave easy access to the grandest scenery at a period when roads were still very poor. Turning to canals, since 1783 the only periods when it has not been possible to board a passenger boat on the Forth & Clyde have been between 1881 and 1893, and between 1939 and 1982.

The other distinguishing feature of Scottish inland waterways is the extent to which their apparent isolation from one another is illusory, in that many have formed parts of through routes which incorporated other modes of transport too. The Crinan and Caledonian Canals were and are far more significant as links in coastal and short-sea shipping routes than for purely inland transport, and even on the Forth & Clyde, despite the prominence of Glasgow, the links with coastal routes at each end were highly important. On the Forth & Clyde the passenger boat services, during their heyday between about 1810 and 1842, were fed by connecting stagecoaches from places such as Stirling, Crieff and, before the Union Canal was opened in 1822, Edinburgh.

At the same period a tourist travelling from Glasgow to Fort William took a Clyde steamboat to Dumbarton, coach to Balloch, steamboat up Loch Lomond to Ardlui and stagecoach from there on. By the end of the century that tourist's grandchildren, travelling to Oban, had a multiplicity of choices apart from the train: these included steamer to Ardrishaig and thence through the Crinan Canal or, if they were not in a hurry, coach from Ardrishaig to Ford and steamer down Loch Awe, at the north end of which it connected with the train to Oban. Such lochs, at that period, served a similar function to branch-line railways: villages beside Loch Tay, for instance, were supplied with coal brought to Loch Tay Pier, Killin, by rail and carried down the loch by barges towed by the steamer.

But links like those have for the most part long since been broken, and the inland waterways have become fragmented. This has been exacerbated by the physical fragmentation of the Forth & Clyde and Union Canals since statutory closure to navigation. Matching this, perhaps, interest in inland waterways has latterly tended to be fragmented too, with attention focused on local projects. This in turn seems set to change with the intended reconnection of the disjointed lengths of the Forth & Clyde and the Union. So I hope this book will appeal to those who would like to see how their own particular bit of waterway fits into the wider context.

Note: approximate metric equivalents have been given in addition to original imperial measurements.

Natural Waterways
Rivers and Freshwater Lochs

Water has been used in Scotland to provide routes for transport since prehistory. The first inhabitants of central Perthshire, for instance, are believed to have arrived on the West Coast and, as they travelled inland, to have made use of the freshwater lochs as an alternative to trackless, wolf-infested forest ashore.

In the first millennium BC many of the inhabitants of Scotland lived on crannogs: artificial islets built of rocks and timber, with timber dwellings upon them. Several hundred crannog sites are known, from Galloway to

A reproduction crannog has been built at Kenmore, Loch Tay.

Shetland, and although some are on small lochs or near the seashore, others are along the edges of the large inland lochs. As a result of recent underwater research, twenty crannog sites have been located on Loch Awe and eleven on Loch Lomond; they are common too on Loch Tay.

Crannogs today, if they appear above the water at all, appear as small islands composed of boulders. How they are believed to have appeared originally can now be seen on Loch Tay where a reproduction crannog has been built, based on the results of excavation of a real crannog nearby.

For transport prehistoric crannog-dwellers evidently used coracles, which are known to have been in use at the time, and dugout canoes or log boats, the remains of which have been found close to several crannogs. Noteworthy are the remains of a log boat discovered in Loch Tay while the reproduction crannog was being built. It was more than ten metres long, made from a single oak tree; once it had a transom stern, and although the transom itself is now missing, the groove to take it was found still packed with moss. Mowat, in *The Logboats of Scotland*, records the discovery in Scotland at one time or another of 154 log boats, most of them at inland locations.

The security offered by crannogs from marauders, both two-footed and four-footed, ensured that their use for strongholds, and for granaries, continued until as recently as the seventeenth century. The comparable security offered by natural islands in the inland lochs appealed to men of war and, equally, to men of peace: the islands became the locations of castles, monasteries, and burial grounds. Such usage implies the use of the surrounding loch as a waterway.

There is however no comprehensive account of the use of inland lochs as waterways: what we do have, drawn from a multiplicity of sources, is in effect a series of snapshots sufficient to indicate just how extensive it was.

Island security was not inviolable: notably in 1263 when the men of King Haakon of Norway's fleet dragged their boats overland across the isthmus between the sea loch at Arrochar and Tarbet on Loch Lomond. The Norseman then laid waste Loch Lomond's islands, which were populous, and the settlements on its shores, and escaped down the River Leven to the Clyde.

By the fourteenth century fleets of large boats or galleys were a feature of Loch Awe. The name of the island of Innis Sèa-ràmhach, off Portinnisherich, is said to translate as 'the Isle of the Six-Oared Galley'; until as late as 1854 the owner of Upper Sonachan had an obligation to maintain a sixteen-oared boat for the use of the Duke of Argyll, or indeed the king.

North of the Highland line there were few if any roads for wheeled vehicles prior to construction of the military roads in the eighteenth century. Travellers and all traffic went on pony-back or on foot – or by boat. That is clear, but precisely what the boats were like is more difficult to establish: the terms used to describe vessels used on Scottish inland and coastal waterways seem seldom to have been used with precision at any period. In the seventeenth century they included galleys and birlinns. The terms may have been partly interchangeable, but galleys were said to have eighteen to twenty-four oars compared with a birlinn's twelve to eighteen. Unlike war galleys, birlinns were beamy: barges for carriage of goods, livestock and people. Both were clinker-built and propelled by square sails (fair winds permitting) as well as oars. Their crews, when rowing, chanted Gaelic songs in time to the strokes of their oars.

W H Murray, writing of the 1680s in *Rob Roy MacGregor: his life and times*, describes the MacGregors' annual September expedition by boat from Inversnaid to Glasgow, carrying the chieftain's rents, and corn, butter, cheese and poultry for sale. The crew sailed or rowed the boat down Loch Lomond as far as Balloch; they then took it down the Leven to Dumbarton, and rowed up to Glasgow with the tide. The return voyage was made with the salt vitally needed to preserve provisions for the winter.

Walter Scott in *The Lady of the Lake* (1810) described the approach of a Highland chief along Loch Katrine at an earlier time:

Far up the lengthen'd lake were spied
Four darkening specks upon the tide,
That, slow enlarging on the view,
Four mann'd and masted barges grew,
And, bearing downwards from Glengyle,
Steer'd full upon the lonely isle;...
Now see the bonnets sink and rise,
As his tough oar the rower plies;
See, flashing at each sturdy stroke,
The wave ascending into smoke;
See the proud pipers on the bow...

This is of course a romanticised view, and there is poetic licence in the terms used, notably 'tide'; but use of oar and sail on the lochs was still commonplace in Scott's day and in essence the description seems accurate.

By the 1830s when this engraving of Loch Oich was prepared, the loch had been incorporated into the line of the Caledonian Canal, and local small boats had been joined by sea-going sailing ships and paddle steamers passing through the canal.

In 1715 the MacGregors, in support of the Jacobites, found it desirable to capture all the boats from the southern part of Loch Lomond and take them north to Inversnaid. This provoked a mixed naval and military expedition in response: pinnaces and longboats from the naval fleet in the Clyde were, with other boats, towed by horses up the Leven and used to carry 700 infantrymen across Loch Lomond from Luss to Inversnaid. But the enemy had gone – however some eighteen of the captured boats were rediscovered although others could not be found.

In the aftermath of the 1715 Jacobite rising, one of General Wade's recommendations was for a fort to be built at the south end of Loch Ness – it became Fort Augustus – and for a small ship with oars and sails to be provided on the loch to supply the fort with soldiers and provisions. 'When she made her first Trip' recorded Edward Burt in *Letters from a Gentleman in the North of Scotland* (written in the 1730s) 'she was mightily adorned with Colours, and fired her Guns several Times, which was a strange Sight to the Highlanders, who had never seen the like before; at least on that inland Lake.' By 1806, though still known as the government galley, this little ship's successor was rigged fore-and-aft as a sloop.

Craft with oars and a single sail are known to have been operating on Loch Shiel in the 1730s. Probably it was in one such that Prince Charles Edward Stewart was rowed up the loch on 19 August 1745 to Glenfinnan. There it was that his standard was raised, and the rising commenced – this must have been due in large measure to its ease of access by waterway.

The fast-flowing rivers of Scotland, though of limited value for navigation generally, were well adapted to transport of timber in the form of logs floated down on the current. Timber from Loch Lomondside was being floated down the River Leven as early as the twelfth century, and it was still being floated down at the end of the eighteenth. At the beginning of the nineteenth century timber was floated down the Tay from Loch Rannoch, down the Aberdeenshire Dee and down the Beauly. But the river used most extensively for this activity was the Spey.

This was largely due to the eighteenth-century activities of that extraordinary undertaking the York Buildings Company, the proprietors of which managed to exploit a joint-stock company, established for London water supply, as a vehicle for speculative ventures in Scotland – notably among the estates forfeited after the Jacobite rebellions but also elsewhere. In 1728 the company purchased 60,000 fir trees on the Grant estate at Abernethy on Speyside and commenced felling on a large scale.

Where logs had previously been floated down the Spey either singly or in small lots, attended by men in curraghs, the York Buildings Company introduced the practice of binding logs together in rafts. Upon these rode the floaters, men equipped with oars, who guided the rafts on their descent. To improve this, a passage was cut through the rocks. The people of the country soon joined the floaters, finding in the rafts a convenient means of transport for themselves and their butter, cheese, skins and other goods.

These commercial activities of the York Buildings Company seem not to have been long-lived, but its timber-floating practices persisted. Elizabeth Grant of Rothiemurchus, in *Memoirs of a Highland Lady*, described the Spey floaters of 1813 thus: 'families by whom the calling had been followed for ages, to whom the wild river, with all its holes and shoals and rocks and shiftings, were as well known as had its bed been dry'. Their day's work was hard, and in their bothy 'they lay down for the night, in their wet clothes – for they had been perhaps hours in the river – each man's feet to the fire,...half stupefied by whisky, enveloped in a cloud of steam and smoke, and sleeping soundly till the morning'.

13

Timber was floated down the Spey over some two centuries, a fact which became important in the 1970s when increasing use of the river by canoeists brought them into conflict with the owners of salmon-fishing rights, who maintained that the Spey was private. The resulting court case, Wills Trustees v Cairngorm Canoeing and Sailing School Ltd 1976, went as far as the House of Lords. The Lords held that the Spey is a public navigable river, and that the right of public navigation could not be lost by non-use. The fundamental requirement for a public right of navigation in a non-tidal river, the Lords held, is that it must be navigable as being suitable for the passage of vessels or rafts so as to provide a means of communication, and that it must be proved that there had been habitual regular use from time immemorial. This became the leading case on the subject: more about it is to be found in the Scottish Rights of Way Society's booklet *Rights of Way: The Authority of Case Law*.

During the 1740s coal was being carried up the River Leven and onward to the head of Loch Lomond for smelting Tyndrum lead ore: the resultant lead was carried away by the same route in reverse. By the 1790s, according to the old *Statistical Account of Scotland*, the River Leven despite its fall of twenty-two feet (seven metres) between Loch Lomond and the Clyde (a distance of about seven miles or eleven kilometres) was considered navigable for half the year for gabbarts and scows. A gabbart was – allowing for the customary lack of precision in terminology – the small sloop-rigged sailing barge of the Clyde and waterways connected with it. On the Leven they were towed upstream by horses and went downstream with the current. The term 'scow' for a large lighter was subsequently closely associated with canals where such vessels were horse-drawn, but at least on the Leven and Loch Lomond some seem also to have been rigged for sailing. By the 1840s, cargoes on the Leven were being transhipped into shallow-draft Leven lighters at times of low water.

The cargoes carried upstream included coal and lime for places beside the river and the loch; after 1790 when the Forth & Clyde Canal was completed, gabbarts carrying coal worked through from the canal to the loch. Down the Leven came cargoes of timber, and slates from Luss. Some twenty years ago the present author was told by the late A J MacFarlane of Balmaha about his grandfather, who traded on Loch Lomond with a sailing scow. One of the principal cargoes was birch wood, from forests on the loch's shores and islands, which was carried down the loch, down the

A sailing gabbart is tracked up the River Leven at Bonhill. SLA

Leven, across the Clyde and up the Cart to Paisley where it was made into bobbins for the cotton industry.

Engravings of the late eighteenth and early nineteenth centuries which depict loch scenes seem almost invariably to include boats, often under sail. Some no doubt were ferries or engaged in fishing but others were carrying goods or people along the loch. By the 1790s boats had for some years carried limestone from a quarry near the head of Loch Earn to kilns near its foot; it was still being so transported forty years later. Dorothy Wordsworth, in 1803, observed on Loch Awe a vessel 'with one large sail spread out, full swollen by the breeze' and conjectured that it had been carrying charcoal for the Bonawe ironworks by Loch Etive.

She was one of many tourists of the period who have left accounts of travel on or beside Highland lochs. Thomas Pennant, in 1772, was rowed down Loch Maree in a six-oared boat. In the 1780s Thomas Thornton sailed down Loch Tay from Killin to Kenmore. In 1803 Dorothy and William Wordsworth were rowed down Loch Katrine by a single ferryman; Coleridge, who was accompanying them, was afraid of the cold in the boat and chose to walk along the shore. Wordsworth, when it began to rain, wrapped himself in the boatman's plaid and slept in the bottom of the boat until his sister, observing ever more beautiful scenery, awoke him. So popular, however, did Scott later make Loch Katrine with tourists that by the 1840s an eight-oared galley, the *Water Witch*, was carrying them. Sir Archibald Geikie in *Scottish Reminiscences* recalled being rowed the length of Loch Katrine in 1843 by four Highlanders who sang Gaelic songs to which they kept time.

The artist Edwin Landseer as a young man was rowed the length of Loch Earn in 1824 en route for the early Highland games at St Fillans. Joseph Mitchell in *Reminiscences of my Life in the Highlands* recalls, also as a young man, sailing up Loch Shiel on a summer morning probably in the 1820s. He and his men landed on Eilean Fhianain to inspect the ruined chapel. But: 'our attention was suddenly directed to a gaily painted boat, which dashed past us down the lake, rowed by four stout Highlanders. In the stern sat a young lady. The boat passed us so abruptly that we stared at the maiden almost rudely; but the suddenness of her appearance and her pretty, graceful manner were a genuine surprise in so solitary a place. Who she was I never could learn.'

The most distinguished person to experience this mode of travel was Queen Victoria, when still in her early twenties and on her first visit to Scotland, in 1842. The high point of this visit was her stay at Taymouth Castle, Kenmore, as a guest of the Marquess of Breadalbane: on leaving she was rowed up Loch Tay for some fourteen miles to Killin.

A D Millar, in his interesting local history *A Bit of Breadalbane*, draws attention to the contemporary account of the event in J Buist's *National Record of the Visit of Queen Victoria to Scotland...* No expense had been spared. The royal barge constructed for the occasion was carvel-built with gold moulding outside, stem head and stern carved and gilt, and painted inside with the Breadalbane tartan. Its length was thirty-two feet, beam six feet ten inches, draught two feet nine inches; it was propelled by eight or ten oars. The rowers' seats were covered with Breadalbane tartan cloth, the royal seat and footstool with velvet, and there were awnings of silk.

On board were the Queen and Prince Albert, the Marquess of Breadalbane, the Duchess of Norfolk and the Duchess of Buccleugh, Captain MacDougal RN, who was chief of the MacDougals and who was in command and steered, two pipers in the bow and sufficient oarsmen to propel the vessel. It was accompanied by four other handsomely decorated barges carrying members of the royal party, and two gigs carrying a military band and more pipers. Of the voyage, Queen Victoria recorded that it was 'the prettiest thing imaginable'.

The Canal Era
the first phase

As early as the 1520s, perhaps earlier, a short canal was built at Upper Largo, Fife, by Sir Andrew Wood. Having retired from a long and distinguished seafaring career, which had included putting to rout the English fleet in the Forth in 1498, Sir Andrew had the quarter-mile canal dug so that he might be rowed in state in an eight-oared barge from his castle to the kirk on Sundays. Its course survives as a depression in the ground.

Sir Andrew was many years ahead of his time. From the reign of Charles II onwards, however, the possibility of making a canal to link the Firths of Forth and Clyde was considered at intervals, but no real progress was made until the wave of enthusiasm for canals which followed construction of the Duke of Bridgewater's Canal from Worsley to Manchester; the first section was opened in 1761.

In 1762 Lord Napier employed Robert Mackell to survey such a canal. Mackell's report was favourable, and in 1763 the Board of Trustees for Manufactures commissioned John Smeaton to investigate the whole question. Smeaton (1724-92) was then the greatest civil engineer in Britain: born in Yorkshire of Scottish descent, he had studied the canals of the Low Countries, and had latterly been engaged on making navigable the Rivers Calder and Hebble in Yorkshire.

Smeaton proposed a canal to run from the Carron to the Kelvin, reaching the Clyde at Yoker; it would be five feet deep (one-and-a-half metres), suitable for the coasting vessels of the Clyde. The lie of the land meant that it would not serve Glasgow: this provoked immediate controversy, for Glasgow wanted a canal, even one of more restricted dimensions, while Edinburgh would have preferred one even larger to take ships from sea to sea. Glasgow merchants employed Mackell and James Watt (who would be remembered as a competent canal engineer even if he had never touched a steam engine) to seek alternative routes for a small canal, but the solution which eventually emerged was for a large one. It was to run from the Forth near the mouth of the River Carron – Grangemouth later grew up at the sea lock – for thirty-five miles (fifty-six kilometres) to Bowling on the Clyde, with a branch of three miles (five kilometres) to the northern outskirts of Glasgow. At the time it was one of the most ambitious canal projects in Britain, for it was to be seven feet deep (two metres) and to have forty locks large enough to take vessels sixty-six feet long (twenty metres) and nineteen feet eight inches wide (six metres). Wooden sailing ships – as all coastal craft were at this period – tended by modern standards to be broad in relation to their length.

For this canal the Proprietors of the Forth & Clyde Navigation (as the company was known) received their Act of Parliament in March 1768. It was a work of national importance. The proprietors included four dukes and six earls, and the Lord Provosts of Edinburgh and Glasgow. They also included Sir Lawrence Dundas, who had made his fortune contracting for

Inland waterways within the central belt of Scotland.

supplies to the army, and across whose estate lay the proposed entry to the canal from the Forth.

Construction commenced that summer at the east end of the canal. Smeaton was chief engineer, Mackell resident engineer. Under them were the contractors, under them again craftsmen such as masons, joiners and blacksmiths, and the 'navigators' – the word was later contracted to 'navvies' – who made up the bulk of the workforce.

The navvies' basic task, once the course of the canal had been marked out, was to dig a channel fifty-six feet wide (seventeen metres) at the top, tapering to twenty-seven feet (eight metres) at the bottom, and to make this watertight. That meant also deeper excavation to make cuttings where the canal was to be below the natural level of the ground, formation of embankments where it was to be higher, and excavation to a greater extent one side than the other where it was to follow the hillside. All this excavation was pick-and-shovel work for muscular navvies: development of mechanised excavating plant lay far in the future.

Meanwhile masons were building culverts to convey burns or streams through the embankments, and aqueducts to carry the canal over rivers and roads. For these and other structures, quarries had to be opened to obtain stone. All the overbridges on the Forth & Clyde Canal were made to open: unlimited air draught was provided for the masts of sailing vessels. Masons built the abutments for neat little double-leaf bascule lifting

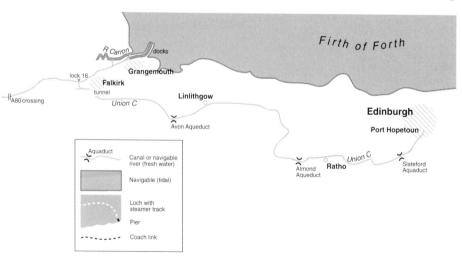

bridges, and joiners and blacksmiths made their decks. Where the canal changed level, the same groups of craftsmen were at work on the masonry of the lock chambers and the timber- and ironwork of the lock gates.

To make the channel watertight, clay puddle was used, to a thickness of two or three feet (one metre). According to J E Handley in *The Navvy in Scotland* the best puddling material was considered to be a lightish loam mixed with coarse sand or fine gravel. Water was mixed with this, and it was chopped about and worked with spades and trampled by strong-booted navvies to produce a homogeneous mass which became impervious or nearly so.

To supply the canal with water, reservoirs and feeder channels were made. A towpath was formed alongside the canal, and a hedge planted to separate it from adjoining land. Wharves and basins were needed, stables for horses and houses for lock-keepers and other employees.

Much of the work was new to Scotland – construction commenced in 1769 of the first lock to be built in the country. By May 1770 over 1,000 men are said to have been at work on the canal. Most came from towns, villages and farms along the route: their numbers fell at harvest time when many men returned to their primary occupation of farming. Navvies were paid one shilling a day, craftsmen one and sixpence; Smeaton, with other responsibilities elsewhere, was getting £500 a year.

Though the largest, the Forth & Clyde was by no means the only canal project in Scotland at this period. In Kirkcudbrightshire, under an Act of 1765, a one-and-a-quarter-mile (two-kilometre) canal was dug from Carlingwark Loch, Castle Douglas, to the River Dee and called Carlingwark Lane. (The word 'lane' is used in that district for a slow-moving watercourse.) It left, indeed still leaves, the loch through a cutting remarkably deep for the period; its function seems to have been partly land drainage, partly navigation. By lowering the level of the loch, beds of marl were exposed and this was then carried by boat to farms up the River Dee and Loch Ken, where it was needed as fertiliser. Another short canal, with at least one lock, was added later to bypass a fast-flowing stretch of river.

In 1767 it was proposed to make the River Forth navigable as high as Aberfoyle, with its lime and slate quarries; and from 1770 onwards there were many proposals for canals in Strathmore and Strathearn. These and many other such projects were destined to remain no more than proposals, for lack of financial support or other reasons. More fortunate were the

The Forth & Clyde Canal near Maryhill, 1852.

promoters of the Monkland Canal, intended to supply Glasgow with coal from the Monklands. An Act was obtained in 1770 and construction commenced with Watt as engineer. Watt became busy elsewhere, too, surveying for canals proposed to cross the Kintyre peninsula in 1771 and through the Great Glen in 1773. A two-and-a-quarter-mile (three-and-a-half-kilometre) canal from Stevenston collieries, Ayrshire, towards Saltcoats Harbour was completed in 1772.

The Forth & Clyde Canal was opened from the Forth as far as Kirkintilloch, whence goods could be carted to Glasgow, in 1773. By 1777 it was open to Hamiltonhill, on the intended Glasgow branch and close to Glasgow itself. The canal rapidly became busy, carrying goods of all types. Regulations published a few years later specify tolls not only for coal, timber and iron but for much else from beef and pork to flour, barley, tin, copper and earthenware. The trades of the butcher, the baker, the candlestick maker were all provided for. Goods were carried in horsedrawn scows, lighters (larger than scows) and coasting craft. These vessels were not owned by the canal company, the function of which was to provide the waterway for others to use. Timber was taken along the canal in rafts towed by horses.

Passengers were carried from 1783 when the company, departing from the usual practice, itself instituted two track boats, the *Glasgow* and the

A pair of horses draw a scow, heavy-laden with timber, along the Forth & Clyde Canal near Camelon about 1930. SLA

Lady Charlotte, to carry passengers and light goods between Grangemouth and Hamiltonhill in a day. 'Track' in this context meant tracked or towed by horses.

The 1770s were years of general financial difficulty and it was only with government aid that work on completing the canal to Bowling on the Clyde resumed in 1786. Robert Whitworth was now the engineer, his principal work the four-arched aqueduct carrying the canal seventy feet (twenty-one metres) above the Kelvin at Maryhill. The canal was opened with ceremony in the summer of 1790; the first vessel to pass through was the sloop *Agnes* making passage from Leith to Greenock with unprecedented ease.

Construction of the Monkland Canal had likewise been interrupted, but the Forth & Clyde Glasgow branch was extended towards it by the 'cut of junction' opened 1791. Upon this lay Port Dundas which became the Forth & Clyde Canal's principal terminal in Glasgow. The Monkland was completed in 1793 (parts had been in use earlier) and provided the Forth & Clyde not only with through coal traffic but also with an additional supply of water. Unlike the Forth & Clyde, but like subsequent canals of purely inland significance, the bridges of the Monkland Canal were fixed rather

The Crinan Canal at Ardrishaig. Among the sailing craft can be seen on the left one of the track boats used to carry passengers along the canal. SLA

than opening ones: the scows which operated upon it were, at this date, horsedrawn and so lacked masts.

In 1792 John Rennie, the noted Scottish engineer whose work lay for the most part in the South, was employed to survey a canal between Loch Gilp and Loch Crinan by the Duke of Argyll and the Earl of Breadalbane. They were now the main promoters of this scheme, previously surveyed by Watt: by enabling ships to avoid going round the Mull of Kintyre it was intended to promote the fisheries and commerce of the West Coast and, in effect, bring them closer to Glasgow by a hundred miles (160 kilometres). An Act for the Crinan Canal was obtained in 1793 and the company formed to build it was not intended entirely for gain. Subscribers included William Pulteney of the British Fisheries Society, David Dale of New Lanark and Josiah Wedgwood, the noted Staffordshire potter who had been prominent in canal promotion in England. Rennie was appointed chief engineer and construction commenced from Ardrishaig to Crinan. The locks were made large enough to take vessels eighty-eight feet long

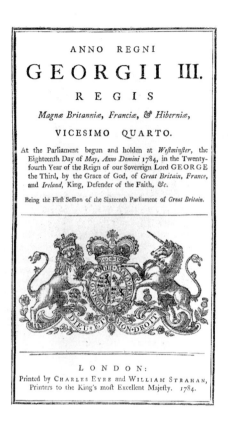

An Act of Parliament of 1784 enabled the government to lend the Forth & Clyde Canal Co £50,000 from the proceeds of sales of forfeited estates.

(twenty-seven metres) by twenty feet beam (six metres).

Rennie also became consulting engineer to the Aberdeenshire Canal: an Act was obtained in 1796 for this canal running inland from Aberdeen, following the valley of the Don, with the intention of providing the transport needed to improve the agriculture of the district.

On the Crinan, problems were encountered with the difficulty of attracting labour to a remote district, the high costs of materials due to the war with France, and the unexpected hardness of the rock. The canal was opened, though not to its intended depth of thirteen feet (four metres), in 1801; the work of improving it went on for years.

Steam pumps, in the form of atmospheric engines in the cylinders of which steam was condensed to produce a partial vacuum, had been in use since the early eighteenth century and James Watt, adding the separate condenser, had improved their efficiency and given them the potential to produce mechanical power. But to use a steam engine to power a ship or boat had long been a dream.

William Symington was one of the first to turn this dream into reality. In 1788 under the patronage of Patrick Miller he fitted a small boat with a primitive steam engine and tried it out on the loch at Dalswinton, Miller's Dumfriesshire estate. The trials were successful enough for a full-size version to be tried the following year on the Forth & Clyde Canal. It ran successfully, but the engine clearly needed much development work, and appeared to contravene Watt's patent.

The NMS model of Symington's pioneer steam boat Charlotte Dundas *which demonstrated her powers on the Forth & Clyde Canal.*

It was only after this patent had expired that Symington resumed his experiments. His patron now was Thomas, Lord Dundas: son of Sir Lawrence, he was governor (chairman) of the Forth & Clyde Canal company and also its largest shareholder. The intention was to produce a vessel to replace horses tracking sailing craft through the canal. Symington eventually designed and built an engine with a simple, original, horizontal layout; this was fitted into a purpose-built hull to drive a stern paddlewheel directly by connecting rod and crank. The resulting vessel, *Charlotte Dundas*, demonstrated her powers convincingly on 28 March 1803 when she towed the sloops *Euphemia* and *Active* over nineteen-and-a-half miles (thirty-one kilometres) in six hours although, as Symington himself put it, 'it blew so strong a breeze right ahead...that no other vessel in the canal attempted to move to windward'. There is a model of the *Charlotte Dundas* in the NMS collection.

Charlotte Dundas was not put into regular service, officially because of fears that her wash would damage the banks of the canal. But the boat

Mr Henderson, lock-keeper, operates one of the Forth & Clyde Canal's locks.

and her creator seem also to have been pawns in a long-running power struggle between Dundas and other proprietors: this was to reach a climax in 1815 when after thirty years Dundas was replaced as governor by Kirkman Finlay MP, the Glasgow cotton manufacturer.

Construction of a canal through the Great Glen had been proposed at intervals during the eighteenth century. By 1800 the Jacobite rising of 1745 and the repressive measures which followed were long past. Highlanders, rather than fighting against the government or amongst themselves, had shown themselves loyal soldiers of the Crown. But although the population had been increasing, the glens were being cleared of their inhabitants to make way for sheep farms. There was much emigration, and loss of a valued source of recruitment. There was also genuine government concern about conditions in the Highlands and, although the situation was complex, one thing was generally agreed: improved communications would be beneficial. Thomas Telford was despatched to the Highlands in 1801, and again in 1802, to report to the government upon conditions and proposed action.

Thomas Telford (1757-1834) was the son of a Dumfriesshire shepherd who trained as a stonemason and went South to educate himself and further his career. About 1787, probably under the patronage of William Pulteney, he was appointed Surveyor of Public Works for the county of Salop with responsibility for its bridges, and in 1790, again at Pulteney's instance, he became surveyor to the British Fisheries Society, which was building fishing settlements and harbours on the coasts of the Highlands. He thus became familiar with Highland conditions, but by no means exclusively for in 1793 he was appointed engineer for construction of the

Ellesmere Canal, acting under the chief engineer William Jessop who had been a pupil of Smeaton. The Ellesmere Canal was a narrow canal for boats of seven feet beam (two metres), but its engineering works were extensive and would eventually include the greatest of all British canal aqueducts at Pontcysyllte.

Telford's principal recommendations for the Highlands were for construction of many new roads and bridges, and of the Caledonian Canal. This would link the east coast near Inverness with, successively, Lochs Ness, Oich and Lochy, and the west coast near Fort William, to provide a route from sea to sea. It would enable ships to avoid the dangerous passage round the north of Scotland (fifty-three shipwrecks in the previous three years); its engineering works would be of necessity large, and would provide much employment for those who might otherwise have been obliged to emigrate.

Separate Parliamentary Commissions were set up in 1803 to oversee, on the one hand, the Highland Roads and Bridges and, on the other, the Caledonian Canal. Chairman of both was the Speaker of the House of Commons; engineer to both was Telford. Construction of the Caledonian Canal was financed entirely by an annual grant from Parliament. In its dimensions, this was to be the largest canal yet constructed in Britain: 110 feet wide (thirty-three-and-a-half metres) at the top, fifty feet (fifteen metres) at the bottom, twenty feet deep (six metres), with locks 170 feet by forty feet (fifty-nine metres by twelve metres). The largest ships trading to the Baltic would be able to pass through the canal, as would thirty-two-gun frigates. For economy, locks were to be built in staircases, that is to say the top gates of one lock chamber formed the lower gates of the next. Eventually staircases were built of four locks at Muirtown near Inverness, of five at Fort Augustus, and of no less than eight at Banavie, near Fort William. The latter, soon known as Neptune's Staircase, meant a continuous masonry structure more than 500 yards (457 metres) long.

Telford's experience at this period was adequate to act alone as engineer for the Roads and Bridges, but inadequate for waterway construction on the scale of the Caledonian Canal. The commissioners consulted William Jessop, his superior on the Ellesmere Canal. Jessop's waterway experience was at that time vastly greater than Telford's: it included construction of the Grand Junction Canal in England and the Grand Canal in Ireland, where he had also surveyed the River Shannon with its loughs. Telford at first welcomed Jessop's involvement, but in later years developed the failing of many self-made men of not giving credit to those from whom he had learnt. Since much of what we know of the early history of the Caledonian Canal comes from Telford sources, it is only recently that the late Charles Hadfield, by diligent research, has been able to show in *Thomas Telford's Temptation* how much of the early responsibility for design and construction of the Caledonian Canal was Jessop's: until 1812 Jessop and Telford acted jointly, with Jessop as the senior, and it was only after that date that Telford was in sole charge.

Despite intentions, canal construction was not wholly successful in providing regular employment for Highlanders, who were accustomed to a working life influenced more by the weather, the season and the length of daylight than by the clock and the regular wage. Nevertheless some 3,000 Highlanders were to find employment on the Caledonian Canal, in relays over the twenty years that it would take to build.

During that period proposals for further canals continued unabated. There were several proposals, for instance, to link the Crinan Canal with Loch Awe, and in 1802 an Act was obtained for the Glenkenns Canal, which would have incorporated Loch Ken into a canal route from Dalry, north of New Galloway, to the sea at Kirkcudbright. Neither was built; but work did commence in 1807 on a long-proposed canal from Glasgow to Ardrossan. No large ship could then reach Glasgow by the Clyde which, despite improvements, was still shallow and it was anticipated that Ardrossan would become its port – but this, as we shall see, was not to happen.

The Aberdeenshire Canal however was opened in 1805. To the lime and coal carried inland was eventually added granite downstream. Passengers started to travel over it in a passage boat in 1807. The edges of the canal were shallow and local residents, remarkably, found them convenient places to do their laundry.

The Canal Era
the second phase

On the Forth & Clyde Canal passage boats, solely for passengers, were introduced in 1809 and the earlier track boats subsequently withdrawn. The new boats were drawn by two horses, changed at intervals; they made the voyage of twenty-five miles (forty kilometres) and four locks between Port Dundas and Lock 16, above Falkirk, in five-and-a-half hours. There were comfortable first and second class cabins with a promenade deck above; meals and drinks were available, draughts, backgammon and a library were provided and a fiddler entertained the passengers. Such a vessel was a welcome alternative to a cramped, bouncing stagecoach and the passage-boat service rapidly became popular. In 1812 44,000 passengers were carried, in 1815 85,368, and numbers went on increasing.

Construction of the Glasgow-Ardrossan canal brought Irish navvies to the district: they settled in Pollokshaws and Paisley. A short section between Paisley and Johnstone was opened in 1810, a longer one between Glasgow and Paisley in 1811. Then work ceased, supposedly as a temporary measure, from shortage of funds. This produced a canal some eleven miles long (eighteen kilometres), known as the Glasgow Paisley & Johnstone Canal or the Paisley Canal for short, with no locks. The latter feature derived from a recommendation by Telford that passage boats should not be delayed, for passenger traffic was expected to be heavy.

Predictions as to passenger traffic proved correct, and goods traffic included all the forms of merchandise to be expected from butter to bricks and, particularly, the cotton goods of the district. Predictions about completion of the canal throughout its intended route would eventually prove less sound: before any of the route was opened an Act had been obtained for further deepening of the Clyde itself up to Glasgow with a view to obtaining a minimum depth of nine feet (three metres).

The eastern section of the Caledonian Canal was opened in 1818; it allowed access from the sea as far as Fort Augustus and was immediately used by coastal shipping. The entrance lock and basin at Corpach were in use from 1819. Robert Southey, accompanying Telford on a tour of

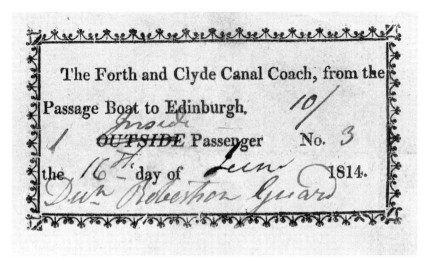

Passenger traffic was important to Scottish canals, and so were links with other forms of transport: the Forth & Clyde Canal offered a through passenger route from Glasgow to Edinburgh by boat to Lock 16 and onward by coach, for which this ticket was issued.

inspection, found great construction activity in the middle district of the canal. He described it in his *Journal of a Tour in Scotland in the Year 1819*. On 16 September at Fort Augustus Telford and he:

> Went before breakfast to look at the Locks, five together, of which three are finished, the fourth about half-built, the fifth not quite excavated…It was a most impressive and remarkable scene. Men, horses and machines at work; digging, walling and puddling going on, men wheeling barrows, horses drawing stones along railways. The great steam engine was at rest, having done its work [of pumping]. It threw out 160 hogsheads [8,400 gallons or 38,000 litres] a minute; and two smaller engines…were also needed while the excavation of the lower locks was going on; for they dug 24 feet below the surface of water in the river, and the water filtered in thro' open gravel. The dredging machine was in action, revolving round and round, and bringing up at every turn matter which had never before been brought to the air and light. Its chimney poured forth volumes of black smoke…The iron for a pair of Lock-gates was lying on the ground, having just arrived from Derbyshire: the same vessel in which it was shipt at Gainsborough, landed it here at Fort Augustus.

Joseph Mitchell was a protégé of Telford and records in his *Reminiscences of my Life in the Highlands* that, as part of his early training as an engineer, he was sent at the age of seventeen to work on construction of these locks. All the masons were from Nairn, or Morayshire; all the labourers were Highlanders. Once Fort Augustus locks were complete he moved west to the lock under construction at Cullochy, where he described how the masons at work there lived:

> I lodged with a party of about thirty in a house built for the lock-keeper. The walls, flooring, roof, and windows were there, but otherwise the house was unfinished...The Men slept in temporary beds one above the other, constructed like the berths in a ship. I was apportioned a closet to myself, lathed but not plastered; my mother sending me food, which I cooked like the rest. The men began work at six a.m....The breakfast hour was nine o'clock, the fare consisting of porridge and milk and thick oaten bannocks about half-an-inch or three-fourths of an inch thick. They dined at two on the same fare, and at eight had supper.
>
> This fare was varied when the new potatoes came in, and fresh herrings were brought down from Loch Hourn in the autumn. On Sundays they luxuriated in tea, oaten bannocks and butter for breakfast... Sunday was reverently kept...the cost of living amounted to 3s. 6d. or 4s. a week out of wages of 21s., each [man] had a very considerable sum to bring home to his wife and family.

Of the Highlanders Mitchell was less polite:

> [They] were not so provident. They lived chiefly on brose, viz., meal in a bowl, a little salt, and hot water mixed into a mess. There was little or no drinking with them here, for there was no public-house within three miles of the place; but at Fort Augustus after a pay-day, which was once a month, the Highlanders took to drinking and quarrelling, and spent then as much money on whisky as would have fed them comfortably the whole month.

But even masons were not perfect:

> At Fort Augustus some of the masons (although very few) could not resist the public-house, and a curious feature of their debauch was that some drank continuously from Saturday till Monday or Tuesday night, without food and without sleep, beyond dozing on the table.

What the Highlanders could achieve on their diet of brose and whisky was observed by Southey at the excavations for the deep summit cutting between Lochs Oich and Lochy:

> The earth is removed by horses walking along the bench of the Canal, and drawing the laden cartlets up one inclined plane, while the emptied ones...are let down another...such a mass of earth had been thrown up on both sides along the whole line, that the men appeared in the proportion of emmets to an ant-hill, amid their own work.

An early paddle steamer takes on passengers at the head of Loch Lomond, looking south.

The Caledonian Canal was opened throughout, though still not at full depth, in 1822. Even while it was being built, a development had taken place which would greatly affect its eventual usefulness: steam propulsion of ships had become fully practicable. Robert Fulton was first to operate a steamship in successful commercial service, in the USA in 1807. Henry Bell brought successful steamship operation to the Old World when he placed his *Comet* in service on the Clyde in 1812. He took her through the Forth & Clyde Canal the following year en route to demonstrate her abilities on the Forth. Sailing vessels could go only when and where the wind, and at sea the tide, could take them: steamships were largely independent of wind and tide, sufficiently so for scheduled services to be introduced. On the Clyde, steamer services grew rapidly and with the deepening of the river itself were sufficient to inhibit completion to Ardrossan of the Paisley Canal.

The first steamer service on a Scottish inland waterway was provided on Loch Lomond by the little paddle steamer *Marion* commencing in 1818. (The date 1817 has generally been given, but R D Campbell writing in *Paddle Wheels*, the journal of the Paddle Steamer Preservation Society, summer 1994, convincingly demonstrated that 1818 is correct.) She was the first of many paddle steamers to ply there, and many of them, like *Marion* herself, were built on the Clyde and taken to the loch, with some difficulty, up the Leven.

A cruise on one of them in 1825 was described by J E Bowman in *The Highlands and Islands: A Nineteenth-Century Tour*. Arriving at Balloch, Bowman and his companions boarded a boat which was poled up the river to the loch where a 'magnificent steam vessel' was in readiness. This proceeded to follow the route which would become traditional for successive paddle steamers over the ensuing 150 years: east of Inchmurrin to pass between Inch Cailloch and the eastern shore at Balmaha, before crossing back to the west shore at Luss and continuing towards the head of the loch. A piper played 'Jacobite tunes and Gathering pibrochs' and Bowman, like innumerable subsequent tourists, was suitably impressed by the gradual revelation of increasingly beautiful and mountainous scenery.

The first regular steamer service on a Scottish canal commenced in 1819 when Henry Bell had *Comet* lengthened and put her into service between Glasgow and Fort William via Crinan. Regrettably she was wrecked late in 1820 but other ships continued the route. In 1820 Bell had arranged for another steamer, the *Stirling Castle*, to be placed in service on the eastern part of the Caledonian Canal between Inverness and Fort Augustus. A coach connection was provided between Fort Augustus and Fort William; then, when the Caledonian Canal was opened throughout, steamers started to operate between Glasgow and Inverness, passing through the two canals en route.

While steam power had been developing there had been independent development which was to have consequences of comparable importance. By 1816 the Forth & Clyde Canal's passenger business was booming, as we have seen, but was liable to serious interruption when the canal froze. Broken ice quickly damages wooden hulls and that autumn the hull of the canal company's committee barge was sheathed with iron plates. Then a design was prepared for a passage boat to be built with its hull made entirely from malleable iron plates.

The boat was built by Thomas Wilson and his blacksmiths John and Thomas Smellie at Wilson's boatyard at Faskine, near Coatbridge on the Monkland Canal. Named *Vulcan* she was launched in May 1819 and went into service in September: the first iron boat built in Scotland, and one of the earliest anywhere. And she was a success.

In 1813 Telford, called in by the government to inspect the Crinan Canal, had reported that it was very imperfect. The canal company could raise no more money: it had already received several loans from the government. This time the government instead made funds available to the Caledonian Canal Commissioners who made the necessary repairs, Telford supervising. In return, the canal became government property until such time as the canal company paid off all its debts to the government. In 1848 the Crinan Canal was vested in the Caledonian Canal Commissioners under the same conditions; it never did revert to the company.

Another canal with which Telford was connected was the Dingwall Canal. This, unusually, was built under powers obtained by the Highland Roads & Bridges Commissioners to build and improve harbours. Yet although tidal it was clearly a canal, about one mile long (one-and-a-half kilometres) and opened in 1817, its purpose to enable coastal shipping to reach Dingwall from the Cromarty Firth. It became Britain's most northerly canal.

Now came construction of the most important Scottish canal of the period. In 1817 – as so often, after several years' controversy over routes – an Act was obtained for the Edinburgh & Glasgow Union Canal, to run from Edinburgh for thirty-one-and-a-half miles (fifty-one kilometres) to join the Forth & Clyde above Lock 16.

The engineer was Hugh Baird, a member of a noted Scottish canal family. His father Nicol Baird, toll collector at the Forth & Clyde Canal's eastern sea-lock, had been promoted to 'surveyor' in 1779 with responsibility for maintenance of the canal wherever completed. Hugh Baird

Overnight boats carried goods and passengers between Edinburgh and Glasgow.

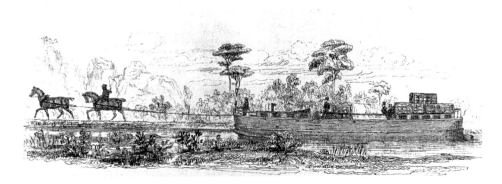

The Union Canal at Ratho, with a loaded scow at the wharf and the Bridge Inn beyond. SLA

succeeded him in 1807 and was appointed 'resident engineer' in 1812. He was appointed engineer for construction of the Union Canal in 1817. His son Nicol Hugh Baird served an apprenticeship on the Union Canal, and then went to Canada to assist Lt-Col John By on construction of the important Rideau Canal. It was the settlement which sprang up around that canal's entry from the Ottawa River which eventually developed into the Canadian capital. The engineering of the Rideau Canal is, in the present author's observation, closely related to that of contemporary canals in Britain, yet By and his military colleagues seem to have played no part in canal construction here: so it is particularly interesting to find this Scottish connection revealed by David Forrester in the Forth & Clyde Canal Society's *Canal News*, December 1996.

The Union Canal saw all the accumulated expertise of half a century of British canal building poured into its layout, design and construction. It was designed as an entity and built at one go: it is to the Forth & Clyde what Edinburgh's New Town is to the Old. To minimise delays to boats, a

The Avon Aqueduct, Union Canal, is the second largest canal aqueduct in Britain.

single long level of thirty-one miles led it from Edinburgh to a point above Falkirk, whence it descended to the Forth & Clyde by a single impressive flight of eleven evenly-spaced locks – a flight, not a staircase, for by then it was appreciated that staircases, though economical to build, were bottlenecks for traffic and wasteful of water. That long level was achieved by a route of sweeping curves, which sliced through high ground by deep cuttings and crossed low ground by tall embankments. Where these could not suffice, the canal with its towpath pierced the hills behind Falkirk by a tunnel 696 yards long (636 metres), and crossed the valleys of the River Avon, the River Almond and the Water of Leith by three magnificent aqueducts. Baird took advice from Telford on the design of these, and as masonry structures with iron troughs they are based to some extent on the aqueduct at Chirk on the Ellesmere Canal: but all are longer and higher than Chirk and the largest, the Avon Aqueduct near Linlithgow, is at 810 feet long (247 metres) and eighty-six feet high (twenty-six metres) exceeded only by Pontcysyllte. And unlike the narrow Ellesmere Canal, the Union Canal and its structures were built to take vessels of 12ft 6in. beam (four metres). The grandeur of its largest structures is matched by the elegant detail of its many smaller ones: it represents British canal-era engineering at its zenith.

The Union Canal was intended from the start to supplement Edinburgh's water supply in addition to providing transport, so arrangements for feeding it with water were extensive. They include a feeder about three miles long (five kilometres) from the River Almond which is an engineering achievement in its own right, with an iron aqueduct over the river and four small-bore tunnels, one of which, provided seemingly where the valley side is too steep for an open channel, is over 1,000 yards long (914 metres).

Highlanders and Irishmen provided most of the navvies on the Union Canal; two of the Irish, Burke and Hare, were to achieve notoriety as murderers and resurrection men. By January 1822 construction was so far advanced – latterly it had been progressed even after dark by the light of blazing torches – that the committee of management was able to inspect the canal by brand-new passage boat from Edinburgh as far as the tunnel. The committee members 'found the banks and bridges thronged with spectators' reported the *Edinburgh Evening Courant* '...testifying delight at this advance of an undertaking...from which the country looks for such immense advantages'. On entering Stirlingshire, the newspaper continued, they were 'hailed by bands of music, flags, bonfires, &c accompanied by the loudest cheers from the multitude...who so crowded...the canal banks that the horses had not room to proceed, and the boat was therefore drawn some miles by the people'. The canal was opened throughout in May.

The Union Canal's Edinburgh terminus was Port Hopetoun, adjacent to Lothian Road. Traffic into Edinburgh soon developed in coal and building materials. Passage boats ran in connection with those on the Forth & Clyde: passengers walked up or down the locks and to shorten the walk the Union Canal was extended past the top of the locks for 570 yards (521 metres); construction of a canal primarily for passenger traffic must have been unusual if not unique. Overnight track boats for cargo were introduced, and from 1824 these also carried passengers, though they still had to change boats.

The NMS collection includes several artefacts relating to the Union Canal. They include a seal matrix with the canal company's seal engraved in agate, a delightful punchbowl decorated with a scene of Port Hopetoun, a booklet of *Rules and Regulations for Traders and Trackers* and a printed list of

milestones and their locations.

In the early decades of the nineteenth century speed of travel first became important. The road improvements of Thomas Telford and John Loudon McAdam enabled the speeds of coaches almost to double, from five mph (eight kph) to nine mph (fourteen-and-a-half kph). Then George and Robert Stephenson developed the steam locomotive to the point at which, as demonstrated on the Liverpool & Manchester Railway in 1829, it could travel at the unprecedented speed of twenty mph (thirty-two kph) or more, and would be able to do so wherever suitable railways were built. Speeds of two-and-a-half mph (four kph) for goods and four-and-a-half mph (seven kph) for

Commemorative china depicting canal scenes was rare, but this detail from a blue earthenware punchbowl in the NMS collection illustrates Port Hopetoun on the Union Canal at Edinburgh.

passengers, in boats drawn by horses clip-clopping along the towpath, suddenly began to seem inadequate.

One evident possibility was to apply rapidly advancing steam-engine technology to canal boats. Steamers with side paddle wheels were now plying regularly through the Crinan and Caledonian Canals but their introduction to the Forth & Clyde Canal and, particularly, the Union Canal with their restricted widths was more difficult. Thomas Grahame, a Forth & Clyde Canal council member, observed how little damage was done to the banks of the Crinan Canal by steamers, and persuaded his fellow council-members to lift the general ban on steamboats on the Forth & Clyde which had existed since *Charlotte Dundas*. The *Cyclops*, an iron passage boat, was modified in 1829 by installation of a steam engine and a single paddle-wheel set within the stern – no satisfactory screw propeller then existed. She went into service between Port Dundas and Alloa, and a much improved version, built by William Fairbairn the Manchester engi-

Lightweight Swift passage boats, drawn by a pair of horses at the gallop, achieved ten miles per hour.

neer, was added in 1832.

William Johnstone, chairman of the Paisley Canal, was also attempting to accelerate its passage boats and in 1830 carried out trials with light 'gig-boat' of the type then used in rowing matches. As Fairbairn described it in his *Life:*

> To this boat he attached two of the track-horses, and, urging them forward at their utmost speed, he found, to his surprise, that instead of a heavy surge rolling along the canal before the boat, the gig rode smoothly over the surface, and the horses actually worked with greater ease upon the collar at the high velocity than they appeared to do at a lower speed. This was...contrary to all received theories...

Evidently the boat was starting to plane.

Thomas Grahame observed the Paisley gig-boat trials but considered the boat too narrow to be stable. A double-hulled boat was built with two gig-type hulls side by side and a single deck mounted upon them with seats for sixty. On trial drawn by pairs of horses in relays this boat travelled from Edinburgh to Port Dundas in six hours and thirty eight minutes which meant an average speed of nearly nine mph (fourteen-and-a-half kph) including locks. She was named the *Swift*, which became the generic name for all the lightweight passage boats which followed.

The original *Swift* when built was, however, considered a step on the

The crew of Carron Company lighter no. 16 pose for the photographer at Port Dundas.

road towards fast steam-propelled boats. But when Fairbairn built a light twin boat of iron with a steam engine, called *Lord Dundas*, the weight of the machinery made her float so low in the water that despite every effort it was impossible to make her plane, and when she was put into service, it was to operate at five mph or so (eight kph).

So it was the next boat to be built, the *Rapid* of 1831, that became in effect the prototype for subsequent swifts: built of malleable iron, single-hulled, length sixty-six feet (twenty metres), beam six feet (two metres), weight two-and-a-half tons, draught, even when fully laden, fifteen inches (thirty-eight centimetres). Horsedrawn, she carried sixty passengers at ten mph (sixteen kph). With such vessels, passenger services were accelerated and made more frequent on the Paisley, the Forth & Clyde and the Union Canals.

Boats of the new type cut the journey time from Glasgow to Paisley from one-and-a-half hours to forty-five minutes, and by the mid-1830s there was a boat every hour through the day: in 1836, no less than 423,186 passengers were carried. The same year 197,710 passengers were carried on the Forth

& Clyde. At this period there were seven boats daily from Port Dundas to Lock 16; thence there were connections by boats on the Union Canal to Edinburgh and by coach to half-a-dozen other destinations. Additionally, there were three boats overnight between Glasgow and Edinburgh, which worked right through. It was probably from the frequent hooting of their horns, to warn bridge- and lock-keepers of their approach, that these swifts became nicknamed, in ornithological pun, 'hoolets' (owls).

In 1839 horsedrawn passage boats were introduced on the Crinan Canal, connecting at each end with coastal steamers which, as steadily larger vessels were built, were already too large to pass through the canal. On 18 August 1847, Queen Victoria passed through the Crinan Canal aboard the passage boat *Sunbeam*, magnificently decorated for the occasion. 'We glided along very smoothly, and the views...were very fine...' she recorded in her *Journal*, 'but the eleven locks we had to go through – (a very curious process, first passing several by rising, and then others by going down) – were tedious...'. A cynic might suppose that she had canal travel in a nutshell!

The depth of the Forth & Clyde Canal had been increased to ten feet (three metres), and the 1830s saw the company at its most enterprising. The improved passenger services were but one aspect of this. There were also boats to carry market carts, and railway wagons, without tranship-ment of their contents; there were experiments with haulage by chain laid along the canal, and by locomotive running along the bank, and, in the 1840s, with screw propulsion. Grangemouth docks were steadily enlarged; Port Dundas became a centre of industry.

There continued to be proposals for further canals, to link Stirling directly with the Forth & Clyde, for instance, and from Balloch to Bowling to link Loch Lomond with both the Forth & Clyde Canal and the Clyde itself.

All this, however, was soon to change with the rapid development of the Scottish railway system, heralded by the opening in 1842 of the Edin-burgh & Glasgow Railway.

Waterways, Railways and Motor Roads

The earliest railways were secondary to water transport. Of simple construction and worked by horse or gravity, they had been used since the mid eighteenth century to carry coal from pit to harbour. Temporary horse railways, much favoured by Jessop, were used from 1805 to move materials for constructing the Caledonian Canal. The committee members of the Union Canal, on their tour of inspection on 21 January 1822, were drawn through their tunnel on a temporary horse railway.

As early as 1812 the Carron Company built a horse railway to link it with the Forth & Clyde Canal. The Monkland & Kirkintilloch Railway, opened in 1826, carried Monklands coal to the canal at Kirkintilloch and so provided a cheap route for coal destined for Edinburgh and the East. It was on this line in 1831 that steam locomotives were first used in regular service in Scotland.

In 1827 the Paisley Canal company obtained powers to complete its proposed line from Johnstone to Ardrossan as a horse railway twenty-two-and-a-half miles long (thirty-six kilometres): but working east from Ardrossan it could raise funds to build only as far as Kilwinning, five-and-a-half miles inland (nine kilometres), and the gap remained unfilled. When a railway was eventually built between Johnstone and Kilwinning, it was not associated with the canal but was part of the Glasgow Paisley Kilmarnock & Ayr Railway opened in 1840. This was a steam railway modelled on the Liverpool & Manchester and so had the advantage of speed. Intense competition followed, between rail and canal, for Glasgow-Paisley passenger traffic. The consequence was that the passenger boats on the canal, so busy so recently, were withdrawn completely in 1843. Freight, however, continued.

That was a matter of local importance. Quite otherwise was opening of the Edinburgh & Glasgow Railway in 1842. Once again there was fierce competition, and on the Forth & Clyde and Union Canals dues for freight and fares for passengers were alike reduced. But despite the safety, comfort and economy which, the Union Canal Co. reminded travellers, were

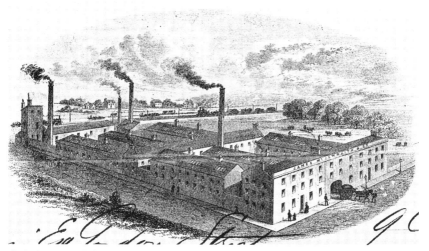

Both the canal and the railway between Glasgow and Paisley appear in the background to this engraving of James McIlwraith & Co's factory, at the head of an invoice of 1875. A few years later the Paisley Canal was taken over by the Glasgow & South Western Railway and much of its route converted into railway. SLA

offered by the swift boats, the passage-boat service between the two cities was withdrawn in 1848. Limited services continued over the Forth & Clyde between Port Dundas and Lock 16, for the towns and villages along the route did not yet have direct rail connection. For freight traffic the canals were in a more competitive position, particularly the Forth & Clyde with its connections with coastal ports.

The mid-1840s were a period of feverish activity in railway promotion and construction. In 1845 the Caledonian Railway received its Act for a railway which, though intended to link the South via Carlisle and Carstairs with Glasgow and Edinburgh, would also in effect produce a second railway between the latter cities. Defensively, the Edinburgh & Glasgow Railway sought amalgamation with three other railways in the region, and with the Forth & Clyde, Union and Monkland Canals. Pending this, these railways and canals were worked as a single group from February 1846. In July the Monkland amalgamated formally with the Forth & Clyde. Then in October the Edinburgh & Glasgow Railway, following a revolt by a faction among its shareholders, repudiated the arrangements for the general amalgamation. Three years later, by which time the Caledonian Railway was open, the Edinburgh & Glasgow Railway did buy the Union Canal. Under the Act of Parliament authorising this, the railway company was to keep the canal in good working order, open and navigable.

The once-impecunious Monkland Canal had, despite some rail competition, become the busiest canal in Scotland for freight. To its coal traffic was added the traffic of the Monklands' booming iron industry. At Blackhill it had a flight of locks: four successive staircases, each of two locks. By the early 1840s the canal was so busy that it was necessary to duplicate the flight. By the end of the decade, when as many as sixty boats were passing the locks in each direction daily, even this was not enough and the locks had to be further supplemented.

This time, to save water and speed up the passage of boats, an inclined plane was built. Such a device had been considered at the beginning of the decade; inclined planes had been installed elsewhere, but not on the scale required. The Blackhill plane was 1,040 feet long (317 metres) with a vertical rise of ninety-six feet (twenty-nine metres) and a gradient of one in ten. Upon it was a pair of railway tracks of seven feet gauge (two metres); on each of these tracks ran a twenty-wheeled caisson large enough for a boat seventy feet long (twenty-one metres) by thirteen feet four inches beam (four metres) to be floated into it at top or bottom of the incline. The caissons were connected by wire ropes to a steam engine at the head of the incline which provided the power needed to move them, although this was minimised by arranging for the caissons to counterbalance one another.

The Blackhill Inclined Plane was brought into use in 1850 and served its purpose well for a couple of decades; then the boom in traffic eased as canalside pits were worked out and the railway network expanded. After about 1887 the plane was no longer used. In the collection of the National Museums of Scotland is an excellent model of it, more than ten feet long (three metres) complete with caissons and gates, which was presented in 1873 by James Leslie who had designed the original: it is displayed in the Museum of Scotland.

Booming coal and iron traffic on the Monkland Canal meant that by 1850 the locks at Blackhill, though duplicated, were inadequate: they were supplemented still further by an inclined plane up which returning empty boats were hauled in rail-borne caissons. Contemporary drawings illustrate the mode of operation of the inclined plane.

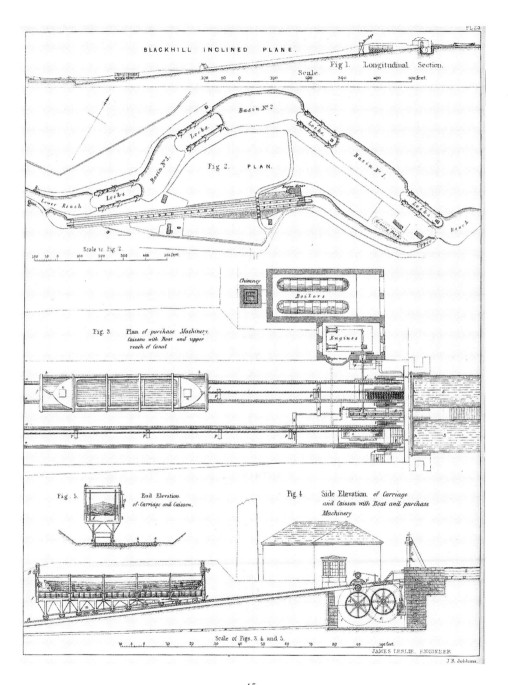

BLACKHILL INCLINED PLANE.

Fig 1. Longitudinal Section.

Scale.
100   50   0   100   200   300   400   500 feet

Fig 2.   PLAN.

Basin N° 2

Locks

Basin N° 3

Locks

Lower Reach

Basin N° 1

Locks

Upper Reach

Graving Dock

Engine House

INCLINED PLANE

Scale to Fig. 2.
100 50 0   100   200   300   400   500 feet

Fig. 3   Plan of purchase Machinery,
Caisson with Boat and upper
reach of Canal

Chimney

Boilers

Engines

Fig. 5   End Elevation
of Carriage and Caisson.

Fig. 4   Side Elevation of Carriage
and Caisson with Boat and purchase
Machinery

Scale of Figs. 3. 4 and 5.
10 5 0   10   20   30   40   50   60   70   80   90   100 feet

JAMES LESLIE, ENGINEER.

J R Jobbins.

45

Freight traffic on the Forth & Clyde was again hauled by horses in the 1850s, for none of the steamers had proved entirely satisfactory. It was with some reluctance therefore that the canal board allowed its engineer James Milne to experiment further by fitting the horsedrawn lighter *Thomas* with a vertical boiler and a small high-pressure steam engine, set as close to the stern as possible to drive a screw propeller.

This time the experiment worked. It was soon found that steam lighters of this type were both technically successful and cost-effective, for two of them could do the work of three similar vessels towed by horses. Within ten years steamers on the Forth & Clyde Canal had grown in number from one to seventy. From these steam lighters was developed the 'Clyde Puffer', small enough to pass through the canal locks but seaworthy enough to trade to coastal harbours and islands. Many were built beside the canal at Kirkintilloch. Even the remaining passage boat on the Forth & Clyde was replaced by the screw steamer *Rockvilla Castle* in 1860. She ran until 1881, by which date railways had reached the most important places she had served.

Grangemouth was served by rail from 1860, when the Forth & Clyde Canal company itself built a branch railway from Falkirk, the nearest point on the railway system. But the 1860s proved to be another period of railway amalgamations. The Caledonian Railway greatly extended its system by acquiring other railways and found that it needed access to an east coast port, particularly for coal shipment. Grangemouth was the most suitable, and to obtain control of it the Caledonian Railway in 1865 took over the Forth & Clyde Canal company and its entire system, canal and rail. In the same year the Edinburgh & Glasgow Railway, and with it the Union Canal, was amalgamated into the North British Railway.

Elsewhere two important Scottish canals were closed and their courses converted into railways: the Aberdeenshire in 1854 and the Paisley in 1881. But on the Forth & Clyde and Union Canals, under railway ownership, traffic just fell slowly away. This was in part due to the rapidly continuing expansion of the railway system into a network that spread like lace over the map of central Scotland, so that within a few decades people generally preferred to send goods by rail. The Caledonian and North British Railways do not seem to have hindered traffic on their canals (as happened on railway-owned canals elsewhere in Britain) but rather to have neglected it. They had little cause to do otherwise: for example, when the Caledonian

Railway carried a load of timber by rail from Grangemouth to Glasgow it profited from providing track and carrying goods; when a load of timber went by canal between the same two places, the railway company profited only from providing the track – the profit on carriage went to the shipowner, with whom the railway was in competition. Between Edinburgh and Glasgow the situation was worse still, for ownership of the canal route had been split between the two companies which had their own rail routes throughout, and over these they competed for traffic: clearly neither had any reason to promote through canal traffic. So although the railway companies fulfilled their statutory duty to maintain the canals, they had no incentive to improve or enlarge them. This lack of investment, as coastal ships grew larger, was to lead to further decline of traffic.

The proposal for a canal from Bowling to Balloch had been overtaken by events, and what in due course appeared was a steam railway between those two points, opened in 1850. Initially it was isolated from the main railway system. Until 1858 passengers came from Glasgow to Bowling by Clyde steamer, and freight by the Forth & Clyde Canal; at Balloch the line terminated at a pier at the foot of Loch Lomond whence steamers continued this mixed rail/water route northwards. Piers at which they could call, eliminating ferry transfers, were built at Balmaha, Luss, Rowardennan, Tarbet, Inversnaid and Ardlui during the late 1840s and early 1850s. From 1847 steamers were able to penetrate a couple of miles (three kilometres) beyond the head of the loch, by means of the River Falloch and a short canal, as far as the coaching inn at Inverarnan.

On Loch Katrine, the first steamer was placed in service in 1843, and shortly afterwards sunk in Luddite reaction, it seems, by the crew of the galley *Water Witch*. A second steamer, launched there in 1846, was more fortunate and became the first of the series which have operated on this loch.

The Caledonian Canal, it will be recalled, had been incomplete when opened, and between 1843 and 1847 it was substantially improved. On the Crinan Canal in 1866 the passage boats were replaced by the little steamer *Linnet* which became a familiar feature of the canal for more than six decades.

Another famous vessel introduced in 1866 was paddle steamer *Gondolier*, which became familiar on the Caledonian Canal for even longer than *Linnet* on the Crinan. In 1873 Queen Victoria embarked on *Gondolier* for a journey through the Caledonian Canal. The queen still found the locks slow and tedious and, with a foot to spare each side, 'nervous work to steer'. No doubt it was, with such a passenger! The queen's collie, Noble, was on board and at one point some of the entourage went ashore to walk the dog along the towpath to the next lock (an activity familiar to a later generation of canallers); at another, when the ship stopped to go through a lock, a poor woman 'came and brought us a jug of milk and oat-cake, which with their usual hospitality the country people constantly offer'.

Both *Linnet* and *Gondolier* carried the mails in addition to their other traffics. They were at first operated, like many other steamers on the West Coast, by David Hutcheson & Co; from 1879 they were operated by one of the former partners in that firm under his own name, David MacBrayne. *Gondolier* is perhaps the best remembered of several steamers used on the Caledonian Canal.

Steamer services commenced on Loch Awe in 1861, on Loch Tay in 1882 and on Loch Shiel about 1893. Other inland lochs upon which steamers of one sort or another are known to have operated include Lochs Maree, Eck, Rannoch, Treig, Arkaig and Morar. Railway stations at piers on inland waterways were opened at Loch Awe in 1880, Lochtay in 1866 (later called Loch Tay: it was at the Killin end of the loch), Banavie (Caledonian Canal) in 1895 and Fort Augustus (Loch Ness) in 1903. Fort Augustus was open for a few years only, but the others lasted for many decades. Loch steamers also connected with trains at Ardlui and Glenfinnan. Railway companies were evidently happy to support waterway transport when it extended, rather than competed with, their main systems. The steamers on Loch Lomond were acquired in 1888 by a subsidiary of the North British Railway, and then in 1896 transferred along with the Dumbarton-Balloch railway to joint ownership by the North British and Caledonian Railways – a unusual instance of cooperation between these companies.

In 1893 James Aitken, whose father had at one time operated the *Rockvilla Castle*, reintroduced passenger steamers to the Forth & Clyde Canal when he placed the pleasure steamer *Fairy Queen* in service. The summer cruises operated by this ship and her successors, all incorporating the word *Queen* into their names, rapidly developed into a popular institution. The route was from Port Dundas to Kirkintilloch and Craigmarloch; the crew were friendly, the ships well-run, one-class only, cheap, and teetotal.

A paddle steamer ascends Fort Augustus locks, Caledonian Canal. SLA

Another vessel which has with the passage of time become a popular institution is ss *Sir Walter Scott*, placed in service on Loch Katrine in 1900. Uniquely among steamers of the period she has survived to remain in service at the present day, meeting the demand for passenger excursions on that loch and at the same time, since she burns solid fuel, ensuring that drinking water, drawn from the loch to supply Glasgow, runs no risk of contamination by oil.

For much of her career the *Sir Walter Scott*'s route between Trossachs Pier and Stronachlachar formed part of more extensive circular tours of the Trossachs. These originated at either Edinburgh or Glasgow and incorporated the steamers of both Loch Katrine and Loch Lomond (Inversnaid-Balloch), with other segments by rail or road as appropriate. But when the *Sir Walter Scott* was new loch steamers were used by far more than tourists. As Mike Troubridge points out in an interesting booklet, *The*

LOCH-AWE.

..CHEAP..

EXCURSIONS

On Wednesdays and Saturdays

DURING APRIL AND MAY,

From Undernoted Stations to

PORTSONACHAN and BACK,

By CALEDONIAN RAILWAY

and the Steamer "CALEDONIA."

GOING.		Return 3rd Class and Cabin.	RETURNING.		
Glasgow (Buchanan St.), Train leaves	A.M. 7.20	7/-	Portsonachan,	Str. leaves	P.M. 4. 0
Larbert, - -	,, 7.55	6/6	Lochawe, -	,, arrives	5. 0
Stirling, - -	,, 8.12	6/-	Do., -	Train leaves	5.15
Bridge-of-Allan, -	,, 8.18	6/-	Killin, - -	- arrives	6.36
Dunblane, - -	,, 8.25	6/-	Balquhidder,	- ,,	6.45
Doune, - -	,, 8.33	5/6	Strathyre, -	- ,,	6.54
Callander, - -	,, 9. 0	5/-	Callander, -	- ,,	7.12
Strathyre, - -	,, 9.17	4/6	Doune, -	- ,,	7.35
Balquhidder, -	,, 9.26	4/6	Dunblane, .	- ,,	7.44
Killin, - - -	,, 9.31	4/10	Bridge-of-Allan, -	,,	7.50
Lochawe Station, Train arrives	11. 4		Stirling, - -	- ,,	8. 0
Do., Steamer leaves	11. 5		Larbert, -	- ,,	8.16
Portsonachan, ,, arrives	P.M. 12. 5		Glasgow (Buchanan St.), ,,		8.55

Luncheons and Teas at Portsonachan Hotel.

Printed at the "Oban Times" Office, Oban.

SS Caledonia *approaches Port Sonachan Hotel, Loch Awe, at the turn of the century.*

Inversnaid Hotel and its surroundings, in those days the Loch Lomond steamers carried not only people but mails, livestock, provisions and even the hotel's laundry hampers. And from an equally interesting booklet, Alexandra Stewart's *The Glen that Was,* it is clear that for the inhabitants of remote Glen Lyon in west Perthshire the route to the outer world lay not via the nearest station at Aberfeldy but by walking or taking a dog cart to Fearnan pier on Loch Tay. Thence a steamer took them up the loch to its head to catch the Killin branch train. At Fearnan, pierman John McPherson had his collie trained to pull the rope for the bell which announced arrival and departure of the steamer: but McPherson was 'gey fond of a drappie' and the tips that this performance produced tended to find their way to the bar across the road.

In addition to the passenger steamers, small cargo steamers carried coal, timber and general cargo on Lochs Lomond, Awe and Tay and

Loch Awe handbill: co-operating with waterway transport, the Caledonian Railway was offering an attractive excursion to Loch Awe at the turn of the century. SLA

possibly on other inland lochs also. A regular service of cargo steamers was operated by MacBrayne between Glasgow and Inverness using the Crinan and Caledonian Canals. The practice arose of building steam lighters for the West Coast trade to a length of eighty-eight feet (twenty-seven metres) able to use the Crinan Canal but not the Forth & Clyde.

The last gabbart to ascend the River Leven is said to have done so in 1874, to the jeers of urchins on the bank to whom no doubt it already seemed old-fashioned. Pleasure craft continued to use the river. The Dingwall Canal was little used by the 1880s, although it remains in existance and its banks are a pleasant walk.

Neither the Caledonian nor the Crinan Canals faced direct railway competition, and by 1907 when a Royal Commission made exhaustive enquiries into canals throughout the UK it appears that traffic was holding up, but that both canals were considered antiquated and detailed proposals were made for their enlargement. Such proposals, made then and at other times, have never had practical result. By 1907 the iron trade on the Monkland Canal had ceased and its coal trade was limited. On the Union Canal, the only traffic exchanged with the Forth & Clyde was the occasional boat-load of road metal, although there was still traffic in coal and bricks into Edinburgh and manure outwards.

P Bonthron, who described extensive travels at this period in *My Holidays on Inland Waterways*, set out along the Union Canal from Edinburgh in a smart white gig, sculling or towing; approaching Linlithgow towards the end of the day he hoisted a sail to take advantage of the breeze. At this point he met a scow: the horse became restive at the approach of Bonthron's ghostly vessel, then turned and bolted. Bonthron eventually managed to get past, at which the boatman prudently called out: 'Are there ony mair o' ye comin'?'

About 160 steam lighters were using the Forth & Clyde Canal regularly, and 170 other vessels. The principal traffics were brought by sea to Grangemouth and transhipped: imported timber still carried in horsedrawn scows, and pig iron, to carry which steam lighters worked round the clock. Don Martin, in *The Forth & Clyde Canal: A Kirkintilloch View*, recorded the experiences of Robert Hendrie who worked on these puffers. Typically a puffer left Kirkintilloch at midnight, arrived at Grangemouth at 5.15 am, loaded pig iron and left about 8.15 am. Glasgow was reached about 5 pm and, after unloading, the puffer left about 9.00 pm to arrive home at Kirkintilloch about 10.45 pm and spend about an hour loading bunker coal before setting out again. Crew members were required to take a rest period of seven to eight hours in bed on board twice a week; the skipper probably only got one.

Coal traffic had largely been lost to rail, but there was still important traffic in general goods between Leith and Port Dundas. The general manager of the Caledonian Railway, giving evidence to the 1907 commission, was at pains to emphasise the difficulties of enlarging the canal.

World War I caused disastrous dislocation to Forth & Clyde Canal traffics: Grangemouth and the Firth of Forth were in effect closed to civilian shipping, which minimised traffic on the canal. The Caledonian Canal was exceptionally busy towards the end of the war, with 5,439 passages recorded in the year ending 30 April 1919 compared with 2,343 for 1913. The cause of the increase was traffic in mine components, brought by sea from the USA to Corpach, transhipped into lighters and carried to Muirtown where the mines were assembled for laying in a barrage across the North Sea, to keep German submarines out of the Atlantic. But this, and other government traffic, paid no dues to the canal commissioners, although some loans were made available.

Passenger services on the Caledonian Canal were curtailed during the war; on Loch Awe and on the Crinan Canal they were for a time withdrawn. Exceptionally, the Queen steamers continued on the Forth & Clyde, their value as rest and recuperation for convalescent wounded being recognised. When the Loch Awe services recommenced in 1922 they were operated by the Caledonian Railway, which likewise came to the rescue of the Loch Tay steamers. In 1923 the Caledonian was absorbed into the new London Midland & Scottish Railway, and the North British into the London & North Eastern; with them went their steamer services and their canals. Meanwhile the Caledonian and Crinan Canals had been transferred to the new Ministry of Transport in 1920.

World War I had also drawn sharply to the public attention the potential for a mid-Scotland ship canal, able to take ocean-going ships, for both commercial and naval use. The proposal had arisen in the late 1880s following the success of the campaign for a ship canal to Manchester, authorised in 1885 and opened in 1894. The most suitable route, it seemed at first, was from the Forth opposite Alloa to the south-east part of Loch Lomond, and then from Tarbet, Loch Lomond, to the head of Loch Long. This immediately produced a reaction in favour of a more direct

TIME TABLE FOR 1915.

DELIGHTFUL AND ROMANTIC EVENING
CRUISES
EVERY TUESDAY, WEDNESDAY, AND THURSDAY.
At 6.30.

Cheap Return Fare, 10d.

Some time at Cadder.

DAILY SAILINGS
per
GIPSY QUEEN
and
MAY QUEEN.
Also

Handsome New Dining and Tea Bungalow, CRAIGMARLOCH.

A panorama of Woodland, Hill, and Dale. Tranquil and Charming. Full of Historical and Commercial Interest. Comfortable, well-fitted and up-to-date Steamers—easy of access from all parts of the City. Four minutes from Normal School Subway and New City Road Cars.

A WHOLE DAY'S EXCURSION.—Sail, Dinner in Bungalow, and DAINTY AFTERNOON TEA on Deck or in Saloon, **3/9**

Leaving Port Dundas Daily at 10.30, Firhill 15 minutes later, Ruchill, 20 mins. later, Lambhill, 35 mins. later.
For Craigmarloch, etc.—Some time ashore; back in city at 6 p.m.
Return Fare, Kirkintilloch, 1s.; Craigmarloch, 1s. 6d.; under 14 years, half-fare; under 6 years Free if with Parents.

Three-Course DINNERS at BUNGALOW, Craigmarloch. 1s. 9d.; JUVENILES (under 14), 10d.

TEAS, Etc., at CITY PRICES, SERVED ON BOARD AT ANY TIME or at NEW BUNGALOW.

Select Afternoon Sail
(except Saturday) Every day at 2.15 through Cadder woods to Kirkintilloch, 1½ hours ashore at Cadder, ½ hour at Kirkintilloch; back in City, 6.15
Return Fare, 1s.

Attractive Saturday Sailings
At 2.15 and 3 p.m., for Craigmarloch, etc., Usual Fares, Guide Book Free. See Diaries also Glasgow Newspapers for Sailings, or alterations. Picnics, Choirs, and Private Parties specially arranged for (with use of Bungalow and Field); also Evening Cruise Charters.

Write for particulars to JAMES AITKEN & CO., LTD., Kirkintilloch.

New Cheap Fare to suit all Classes. Every Monday, Single Fare Day at 10.30, all day Sail, 1/- Afternoon Sail at 2.15, 8d. return. Return Steamer back in City, 6.10.

route from Grangemouth via Kirkintilloch to Yoker, and this in turn produced an extended controversy over routes in which the possibility of following the Vale of Leven from Loch Lomond to the Clyde also became a factor.

It was all reminiscent of the controversy a century earlier over routes for the the Forth & Clyde Canal, but this time without practical result, usually on grounds of cost. Schemes were considered during and after World War I and in the 1940s. In 1976 the newsletter of the Scottish Inland Waterways Association reported a proposal for a Forth-Clyde canal to take 1,500 ton capacity vessels, linking the inland waterways of the Continent with an ocean terminal on the Clyde, and there was another proposal as recently as 1995.

It is certainly the opinion of the present author that if the Forth & Clyde Canal company had escaped railway takeover, as did the Aire & Calder Navigation further south, then like the Aire & Calder it would have steadily improved its canal to take larger and larger vessels. By the present day the canal might well have been enlarged sufficiently to take low air draught Rhine-Sea ships, such as those which come up the Firth of Tay to Perth harbour over thirty miles (fifty kilometres) from the open sea. Straight through by water from Düsseldorf to Port Dundas: it is an intriguing thought.

Such speculation is also unfortunately to rewrite history, and we must now return to reality and the period following World War I. As early as 1912-13 a fleet of eight lighters equipped with internal combustion rather than steam engines was built at Kirkintilloch in an attempt to improve the economics of such vessels, by reducing machinery space and increasing the space for cargo. But this promising development seems to have foundered in World War I. The general application of internal combustion engines to vessels using Scottish inland waterways did not come for another two or three decades. Rather, the 1920s saw rapid growth in motor road transport and associated road improvements; it is a trend which has continued to the present and from about 1927 the railway system too started to contract. In the 1920s both waterways and railways found them-

Aitken's pleasure cruises on the Forth & Clyde continued during World War I: their value was recognised as rest and recuperation for overtired industrial workers on war work, and for convalescent wounded soldiers.

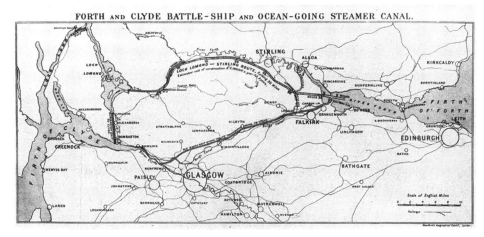

One of many schemes for a Mid-Scotland ship canal. SLA

selves facing this new competition at a time when traffic was in any event badly hit by industrial depression. The Forth & Clyde never recovered fully from loss of traffic in World War I.

Winter steamer services on Loch Tay ceased in 1925, and on Loch Lomond in 1933. In 1929 MacBrayne replaced the Crinan Canal steamer, and also the Crinan-Oban steamer, by a motor coach running direct between Ardrishaig and Oban.

The Union Canal in Edinburgh had for long seemed redundant, and in 1912 an agreement had been made between Edinburgh Corporation and the North British Railway by which Port Hopetoun and its approach were to be filled in and the land either built over or used for street improvements; quays were to be provided at the new termination of the canal. The war had intervened, but Port Hopetoun was closed in 1921 and filled in. Further contraction occured in 1933 when the London & North Eastern Railway began filling in the locks connecting the Union Canal with the Forth & Clyde, under powers obtained in 1930. The canal remained important for water supply to industry. Traffic on the Monkland Canal ceased about 1935, but it too continued to be important for water supply, not least to the Forth & Clyde. In the 1930s some improvements were made to the Crinan Canal, and the London Midland & Scottish Railway built three new motor vessels for its inland waterway shipping routes, one of

56

Houseboats were popular on Loch Lomond and the River Leven in the 1930s. SLA

them being *Countess of Breadalbane* in 1936 for Loch Awe (the other two were for Windermere).

World War II however brought about suspension of the passenger steamer services on Loch Awe, Loch Tay, the Forth & Clyde Canal and the Caledonian Canal. The hull of the *Gondolier* came to an ignominious end as a block-ship in Orkney.

The year 1948 brought the general nationalisation of transport. So far as inland waterways in Scotland were concerned, the effect was that canals, docks and ships belonging to railway companies were transferred to the newly established British Transport Commission, and so were the Caledonian and Crinan Canals. The Monkland Canal, however, was statutorily closed to navigation in 1950; most (but not all) of it was subsequently filled in and piped, and its course used for the M8 motorway. Loch Tay steamer services were not resumed, and the sole surviving steamer was cut up at the lochside in 1950.

The Loch Awe service had recommenced in 1948 with the *Countess of Breadalbane*. But too few passengers presented themselves, and after the end of the 1951 season the service was withdrawn and the ship taken to the

Puffers in Crinan Basin, Crinan Canal. SLA

Clyde. The same year the service on Loch Shiel, between Acharacle and Glenfinnan, was taken over by MacBrayne and operated by two motor vessels. It included carriage of mails, and was continued until 1967 when a new road was built and the mails transferred to road. Locally-owned mv *Rose Isle* subsequently carried passengers up and down the loch.

A new mailboat service had been established in 1948 on Loch Lomond when A J MacFarlane was awarded the contract to carry mails from his boatyard at Balmaha to the inhabited islands of the loch. The vessel principally used, then and now – for the service continues to operate – is the teak-hulled motor launch *Marion*, named after the loch's earliest steamer. Passengers are carried too: it is an enjoyable excursion.

The full flavour of life aboard Loch Lomond steamers in the early 1950s is recalled by Duncan Graham in his delightful book *Sunset on the Clyde*. As a student on vacation he worked as assistant purser on the paddle steamer *Prince Edward* of 1911. Duties ranged from the official one of coping with an immense range of tickets – for passengers joining the ship at piers up the loch demanded, and were issued with, tickets not just to Balloch but to railway stations far and wide beyond – to the unofficial one of writing, on behalf of a crew member who was unable to perform this task for himself, letters to the wife left behind on the croft on Skye.

In 1950 the nationalised transport undertaking ordered a new steamer for Loch Lomond and this, *Maid of the Loch*, was launched in 1953: the last traditional paddle steamer built for use in Britain and the largest ship built for use on the loch, 191 feet long (fifty-eight metres) and authorised to carry 1,000 passengers. From 1955 she operated the service alone, and by the 1960s she was operating at a loss, although popular with passengers.

Use of the Crinan Canal by cargo ships and fishing boats continued to decline during the 1950s and 1960s, while its use by yachts increased. By the mid 1960s shipowners trading between the Clyde and the Western Isles were no longer finding it economic to use ships small enough to pass through the Crinan Canal and were building larger ones, despite the need to send them round the Mull of Kintyre. The Caledonian Canal in the 1950s was being used mostly by fishing craft and also by small cargo ships. A programme of mechanising the lock gates commenced in 1960 and the

SS Queen of the Lake, *Kenmore, Loch Tay.* SLA

59

As late as 1961 the puffer Anzac, *by then already diesel-powered, visited Port Dundas - probably to unload whisky from Islay.*

same year the canal tug and icebreaker *Scott II* was adapted to carry passengers so that passenger trips from Inverness could be reintroduced.

By the 1950s, as ships the size of puffers were becoming too small to carry economic loads, except in specialised circumstances, use of the Forth & Clyde Canal for trade became minimal. It was, however, still used by fishing boats and yachts en route from one coast to the other. Its bascule bridges were narrow and weak, and some had been replaced by wider, large-span powered lifting or swing bridges: the expense of installing and operating these was, at least in some instances, borne by the local authorities. The NMS reserve collection includes a large-scale working model of the powered single-leaf bascule bridge installed at Temple in 1932 to carry Bearsden Road over the canal. Unfortunately, the motivation for installing such bridges was to improve the road system rather than the waterway. Even so, when opened they held up busy road traffic. The water was dirty and strewn with rubbish: there were, regrettably, many cases of drowning. Public opinion, reflected by local-authority policy, came to see the canal as an anachronism, a hindrance to use and expansion of the road system, a danger to life and health. The decision to close it was taken by the British Transport Commission in 1961, and on and from 1 January 1963 the Forth & Clyde Canal was statutorily closed to navigation. The immediate cause was to avoid construction of a new £160,000 swing bridge for the improved A80 road. Only the basin at Bowling remained open, to provide moorings off the Clyde. The Union Canal went the same way, and was statutorily closed in August 1965.

Meanwhile the nationalised waterways had been transferred to the newly established British Waterways Board under the Transport Act 1962.

Recreation and Revival

What those who had demanded closure of canals seem to have failed to appreciate was that closing a canal to navigation did not instantly remove it from the face of the earth. To eliminate a canal, that is to drain it, fill it in, and make all the structures safe was, except in special circumstances, prohibitively expensive. Besides, there were long-term commitments to water supply which, if broken, would require compensation and, if continued, piping.

So what happened was that in a few places – such as Wester Hailes on the Union Canal and Grangemouth on the Forth & Clyde – the canal was filled in, and on the Forth & Clyde the water level was lowered by some three feet to reduce maintenance expense. Generally, opening bridges were fixed and bridges which obstructed road traffic to excess were demolished and replaced by embankments, through which canal water was conveyed by pipes. The canal approaches to these piped crossings became places for floating weed and rubbish to collect; locks were maintained only sufficiently to retain water in the canal above, so that the lower gates gently disintegrated, while rubbish accumulated in the chamber; and such half-derelict canals were no more proof against drownings than canals in use.

As things turned out, the closures of the Forth & Clyde and Union Canals were among the last closures of canals of consequence anywhere in the British Isles. Elsewhere, at the time they were closed, the tide was already flowing strongly in favour of waterway restoration. In 1964 for instance the Queen Mother ceremonially re-opened the Stratford Canal, restored from near-dereliction. This was in turn a consequence of the postwar rediscovery of the neglected canals and inland waterways by the public. It had prompted, and had then been much encouraged by, formation of the Inland Waterways Association in 1946 to campaign for the retention and use of British inland waterways. The Inland Waterways Association of Ireland was formed in 1954 with comparable aims. 'Use' meant all forms of use, pleasure traffic as well as commercial, and pleasure traffic on the inland waterways of England and Ireland began to increase.

After the Union Canal was closed to navigation in 1965 it was obstructed by piped crossings such as this one near Polmont. The canal continues beyond the road.

Parliament, reflecting both the IWA's campaign and the shift in public opinion, reclassified the waterways of the British Waterways Board, in the Transport Act 1968, under three headings: commercial waterways, to be 'principally available for commercial carriage of freight'; cruising waterways, to be 'principally available for cruising, fishing and other recreational purposes'; and the remainder, to be 'dealt with in the most economical manner possible (consistent, in the case of a waterway which is retained, with the requirements of public health and the preservation of amenity and safety), whether by retaining and managing the waterway, by developing or eliminating it, or by disposing of it'. Regrettably, the same Act abolished the public right of navigation over the Board's waterways.

The Caledonian and Crinan Canals were classified as commercial waterways, and the Forth & Clyde, Union and Monkland Canals became remainder waterways. This remains in essence the position early in 1999; the British Waterways Act 1995, however, gave British Waterways statutory responsibilities towards the environment, both built and natural.

No waterways in Scotland have been classified as cruising waterways, even though the recreational value of inland waterways has been appreciated better, and for longer, in Scotland than in most other parts of Britain. The Union Canal was advertising pleasure trips from Port Hopetoun to the Almond aqueduct as early as the 1830s and many other instances of recreational use, such as the *Queen* steamers on the Forth & Clyde, have been mentioned in earlier chapters. Perhaps it was because the canals and lochs were too familiar that Scotland during the 1950s and 1960s lagged behind England and Ireland in appreciation of inland waterways for their own sake. A laudable attempt by British Waterways to operate two small hire cruisers on the Union Canal in 1959 lasted only two years, for sufficient customers did not appear. It was not until 1970 that hire cruisers were introduced to the Caledonian Canal, and that event owed much to appointment as chairman of the Highlands & Islands Development Board of a former British ambassador to the Irish Republic, Sir Andrew Gilchrist, who had observed the growth of hire cruising on the Shannon. It proved successful on the Caledonian Canal too: in 1998 some 150 hire craft, motor cruisers and sailing vessels, were on offer.

Likewise it was not until 1971 that the Scottish Inland Waterways Association was formed. It originated from a conference at Edinburgh University on the future of the Union Canal convened by Basil Skinner: Skinner had been prominent in successful opposition to proposals by Stirlingshire County Council to fill in several miles of the canal and turn it into a road. The principal object of SIWA was to advocate the restoration, maintenance, development and use by commercial and pleasure traffic of all inland waterways in Scotland.

Against a background of continuing proposals to fill in parts of the Union and Forth & Clyde Canals, SIWA made a start by organising working parties of volunteers to clean up the canals and rallies of small boats to use them. In July 1973 came a race for powered inflatable boats (five horsepower maximum) from Wester Hailes right through to Glasgow, with the boats portaged past obstructions: it was the forerunner of many subsequent marathons for inflatables. The biggest step forward, however, came at the end of 1974 when the restaurant boat *Pride of the Union*, sixty-five feet long (twenty metres), was placed on the Union Canal at the instigation of Ronnie Rusack of the Bridge Inn, Ratho. This meant that the canal once again had a full-size boat in operation. In 1978 Bonnington Aqueduct, between Ratho and the Almond Aqueduct, required rebuilding: the work was done to navigable standard. The following year, after several years' controversy, it was decided that an aqueduct would be built at Sighthill to carry the canal over the planned Edinburgh bypass. Meanwhile, on the Forth & Clyde when Glasgow Bridge, Kirkintilloch,

Over 5,000 disabled and elderly passengers enjoy free cruises on the Union Canal each year on St John Crusader *and* St John Crusader II *organised by the Order of St John and Seagull Trust Cruises..*

was rebuilt in 1975 a large-diameter culvert, with room for small boats, was installed.

Paradoxically, 'remainder waterway' status, which reduced to the minimum the standard of maintenance required by law of British Waterways, had the effect of opening the door to financial and practical support, by local authorities and voluntary groups, for something better. In 1976 the Union Canal Development Group, composed of representatives of local authorities, the Countryside Commission for Scotland and British Waterways, recommended that nothing further should be done to impede eventual restoration of the whole canal and called for removal of obstacles to navigation.

In 1976 the Scottish Inland Waterways Association, through its vice chairman Rev P H R Mackay, investigated the possibility of providing barges for handicapped people, along the lines of those then recently introduced on the Montgomery Canal and on waterways in Nottinghamshire. This would meet the dual aims of encouraging use of canals and alleviating the difficulties experienced by the handicapped. The

Former Clyde ferry Ferry Queen *is launched into the Forth & Clyde Canal in 1982 to revive passenger cruises.*

outcome was the formation of the Seagull Trust, with assistance from the Edinburgh Order Committee of the Order of St John, to provide cruises for the disabled and elderly. The first boat, *St John Crusader*, entered service on the Ratho length of the Union Canal in 1979, and was so successful that it was soon followed by four others on the Union, Forth & Clyde and Caledonian Canals.

Establishment of SIWA was followed by formation of many local canal societies, particularly along the Union and Forth & Clyde Canals, the better to address local problems with local support. Notably, the Linlithgow Union Canal Society had been formed in 1975: it opened Scotland's first canal museum in former canal stables and from this base began to operate trip boats on the canal.

The Forth & Clyde Canal Society was formed in 1980. Almost immediately it acquired a redundant example of the once-familiar Clyde ferries, and in 1982 used it to reintroduce regular passenger trips on the canal. The section concerned was between Kirkintilloch (Glasgow Bridge) and Bishopbriggs, formerly part of the route of the *Queen* steamers, so it was perhaps with a degree of inevitablity that the new trip boat was named the

Ferry Queen. She quickly had company at Glasgow Bridge, for the former canal stables there had in 1981 been converted into The Stables restaurant, which added to its facilities the cruising restaurant *Caledonian*, converted from another Clyde ferry.

From about 1980 the Scottish Inland Waterways Association took on the comparatively low-key role of national umbrella organisation. In 1984 it organised an excellent national conference addressed by the chairman of British Waterways Board, and in 1996 a canal festival at Wester Hailes.

A barrage was built across the River Leven at Balloch in 1971, under powers given in 1966 to impound the waters of Loch Lomond for use as water supply. No lock was provided, but slipways were installed immediately upstream and downstream of the barrage to enable boats to pass it, as they have done from time to time. The railway to Balloch Pier was electrified in the early 1960s as part of the Glasgow suburban network. Little advantage seems to have been taken of the line's potential for excursion trains from further afield although (in the author's view) to fill a ship the the size of *Maid of the Loch* demanded passengers by the trainload. There was some praiseworthy publicity for the loch steamer, but her operation was also hampered by successive closures of the piers up the loch, which were not owned by the steamer operator. Inverarnan was by then ancient history having closed in the 1870s; Luss pier was closed about 1949 and Ardlui in 1964, to be followed by Balmaha in 1971 and Tarbet in 1975. That left only Rowardennan and Inversnaid for the ship to call at, although the round tour including the Loch Katrine steamer was still on offer at £3.15, second class, from Glasgow back to Glasgow.

Luss pier, however, was taken over by Strathclyde Region, rebuilt and re-opened for the 1980 season. But at the end of the 1981 season *Maid of the Loch*'s operator Caledonian MacBrayne withdrew the ship from service and put her up for sale: despite increasing traffic, and local authority subsidies, the loss on operating was too great.

The purchaser was Alloa Brewery Co Ltd, a subsidiary of Allied Lyons plc, which intended to use the ship as a static restaurant as well as for cruising, and to pursue related developments ashore. To maintain the service up the loch, it purchased another vessel: no less than mv *Countess of Breadalbane*, formerly of Loch Awe, which it renamed *Countess Fiona* and brought from the Clyde to Loch Lomond in time for the 1982 season. With a capacity for 180 passengers and a crew of six (compared with *Maid of the*

Waterborne mail service: A J MacFarlane carried the mails to Loch Lomond's islands.

Loch's thirty-three) *Countess Fiona* covered her costs without subsidy, but the paddle steamer lay out of use and deteriorated. Then in 1986 financial support for the railway to Balloch Pier was withdrawn by Strathclyde Passenger Transport Executive despite its having, I believe, a duty to promote integrated transport. The rail/water route was then broken by closure of the 600 yards (550 metres) of railway between Balloch Central and Balloch Pier.

In 1989 Alloa Brewery sold the two ships to new owners with ambitious plans; they formed Maid of the Loch Ltd and operated *Countess Fiona* during the summer of 1989. Her calls up the loch were at Balamaha, re-opened that year, Luss, Rowardennan, Tarbet (re-opened 1984) and Inversnaid. But in 1990 sailings were suspended; there were financial problems at the parent company and by the summer Maid of the Loch Ltd was in receivership. The two ships were sold yet again to Francis Leisure Group, which intended property development at Balloch Pier but in turn went into liquidation early in 1992; shortly before this watchmen on *Maid of the Loch* had been dismissed and many valuable components were stripped out of the ship, while so much rainwater entered through the leaking superstructure and accumulated in the bilges that it was in danger of sinking.

This sorry tale of the decline of the shipping service which gave access to what is probably Scotland's best-known loch, an internationally famous attraction for tourists, is scarcely credible. It was in marked contrast to the continuing success of comparable lake shipping services elsewhere, such as those in Switzerland. Fortunately it was not being matched elsewhere in Scotland either. On Loch Awe passenger trips were revived in 1986 by Harry Watson, who formed the Dalriada Steam Packet Co Ltd. The vessel used was the steam launch *Lady Rowena* and the service was based on the pier at Loch Awe station which had itself been re-opened the previous year after closure since the 1960s. Most trips were short-distance, but on occasion *Lady Rowena* plied up the loch as far as Port Sonachan and Dalavich. She was later joined by mv *Flower of Scotland*. On Loch Katrine, replacement boilers were installed in ss *Sir Walter Scott* in 1991 to give the ship a new lease of life.

Canal restoration spread during the 1980s to that most unlikely of candidates, the Monkland Canal. Coatbridge, former boom town, was suffering extreme urban dereliction; to alleviate it, Monklands District Council brought in consultants, Land Use Consultants by name. In consequence a walkway four miles long (six-and-a-half kilometres) was made on the course of the filled-in canal, two lengths of canal were re-excavated and filled with water, and a surviving one-and-a-quarter-mile (two-kilometre) length through Drumpellier Park, west of the town, was dredged, tidied up, and provided with a slipway for small craft.

Beside the re-excavated canal the derelict site of former blast furnaces was redeveloped as an open-air industrial museum, Summerlee Heritage Park. Features included reconstruction of a canalside boatbuilding yard. Running in parallel was a scheme to construct a full-size replica of *Vulcan*, the 1819 iron-hulled passage boat. The replica was built to the order of Monklands District Council in 1988 to provide work for unemployed ship-building craftsmen. Mild steel had of necessity to be used for the hull, but the builders were able to revive the techniques of rivetting it together. The replica *Vulcan* was shown at Glasgow Garden Festival and then moved to Summerlee for permanent display.

Of the Paisley Canal too a short length survived, through the Ferguslie thread works at Paisley. The Paisley Canal & Waterways Society was formed in 1988 to preserve it: although the thread works has been demolished, the canal is, in 1998, being landscaped as housing is built around it.

On the Caledonian Canal the spectacle of sailing ships en masse reappeared in 1991 when more than forty-two passed through it, competitors in the Cutty Sark Tall Ships Race.

Rapidly increasing quantities of pleasure craft were a feature of some lochs, with power boats and sailing craft coming into conflict with each other and with other loch users, as at Loch Ken. The River Dee had been impounded at Glenlochar, several miles below the loch, in 1935 in connection with the Galloway hydroelectric scheme. This raised the water level in the river to that of the loch and in effect produced a loch some nine-and-a-quarter miles long (fifteen kilometres). By the 1970s this was proving very attactive to pleasure craft and in the 1980s Dumfries & Galloway Region introduced regulations to cover, principally, zoning of the loch and registration and insurance of boats.

The 'Friends of Loch Lomond', a charitable voluntary organisation, was formed in 1978. Its objects are to protect, conserve and enhance the loch and its surroundings, so its concerns include navigation. The Loch Lomond Association, a water users' association, was formed in 1981. It produced a voluntary code of conduct, but this had limited effect as was shown dramatically in 1993 when two power boats collided after dark in a tragic fatal accident. According to press reports, one of the drivers was unaware of the code. Byelaws to cover boat registration and navigation on Loch Lomond were eventually introduced in 1996 by the local authorities acting through their joint committee, the Loch Lomond Park Authority. They were made under section 121 of the Civic Government (Scotland) Act 1982. Since the Act omits powers to demand third-party insurance of boats, or to charge for registration, and provides for regulation of pleasure craft only, not commercial vessels, it appears that amendment is desirable. The first year of registration produced 4,300 registered boats, and their numbers have since rapidly increased.

A vessel which it is hoped will soon be joining them in action is paddle steamer *Maid of the Loch*. Dumbarton District Council came to the rescue in 1992, initially with emergency measures to ensure security and pump the bilges, and subsequently by purchasing the ships *Maid of the Loch* and

Paddle steamer Maid of the Loch *is being restored at Balloch Pier, Loch Lomond.*

Countess Fiona, with Balloch pier and adjoining land. In 1993 a consultants' study favoured return of *Maid of the Loch* to full steam operation at an estimated cost of over £2 million. It was recommended that she should become a 'flagship cruising experience', with operational capacity reduced to 500 passengers; it was also, regrettably, in the author's opinion, recommended that if restoration of the Maid went ahead, *Countess Fiona* would not have a future on the loch.

Working parties of Paddle Steamer Preservation Society volunteers went aboard the *Maid of the Loch*, initially for a temporary clean-up which rapidly evolved into regular weekly occasions working on restoration. Externally the ship was repainted down to the waterline, in a handsome black, white and red livery; internally from deck to bilge skip-load after skip-load of rotting debris was removed. In December 1995 ownership was transferred by Dumbarton District Council to the Maid of the Loch Trust, and then passed on during 1996 to the the Loch Lomond Steamship Company Ltd, a charity formed by the trustees. The pier, land and *Countess Fiona* passed to West Dunbartonshire Council which put *Countess Fiona* up for sale.

Preston Road bridge on the Union Canal, piped for many years, was rebuilt in 1992 fom a piped crossing, and enables Linlithgow Union Canal Society electric trip boat to pass beneath en route for Avon Aqueduct.

The *Maid of the Loch*'s hull was sound but her boiler had deteriorated beyond repair: it was cut up and removed piecemeal. A replacement deck in steel was installed, and with that and a cap over the funnel the interior was finally made weatherproof. An open day in 1997 attracted over 2,000 visitors. Industry was generous. Funding was sought from lottery, European and other sources. Loch Lomond Park Authority made a parallel bid for lottery funding to restore the piers at Balloch, Luss, Tarbet and Balmaha. By the winter of 1997 the charitable company's stated aims were to return *Maid of the Loch* to steam operation with new boiler or boilers and improved accomodation, and to provide full-length and cross-loch sailings from Easter to September with reduced services in spring and autumn.

The Forth & Clyde and Union Canals have been coming back to life at a steadily increasing pace. A big step forward was the Glasgow Canal Project announced in 1986 to reopen twelve miles (nineteen kilometres) of the Forth & Clyde Canal. That did not mean, however, reinstatement of unlimited air draught: where culverted bridges were rebuilt, fixed bridges were to be provided with a minimum of three metres headroom (ten feet). This was in accordance with the planning guidelines in the Forth & Clyde Canal Local Plan, which the local authorities along the canal had prepared in conjunction with British Waterways; it was adopted in 1988. By 1989 there were six trip boats operating on the canal.

On the Union Canal 1992 saw the piped crossing at Preston Road, Linlithgow, rebuilt as a bridge: this enabled trip boats from Linlithgow to cruise to the Avon aqueduct. The Linlithgow Union Canal Society added the electrically-powered forty-seat trip boat *St Magdalene* to its fleet in 1995. Activity at Ratho has steadily increased, with the Bridge Inn becoming the focal point of the Edinburgh Canal Centre, and a second restaurant boat and the vintage passenger launch *Ratho Princess* added to the fleet. The Seagull Trust also brought in an additional boat at Ratho, and then in 1996 replaced the original one by *St John Crusader II* built by Greentours Ltd of Daventry. In 1997 6,500 disabled and elderly people and their carers enjoyed free cruising.

The Avon aqueduct had been scheduled as an ancient monument in 1966, and the Kelvin aqueduct in 1968. Numerous other canal structures were scheduled subsequently and by 1996 the entire Union, Crinan and Caledonian Canals were scheduled. The Forth & Clyde Canal incorporated some eighty-five scheduled ancient monuments.

In 1991 it became known that the Scottish Development Department's preferred option for further upgrading the A80, for which 1960s improvements had prompted closure of the Forth & Clyde Canal, was to build a new motorway roughly parallel to the road: this would cross over the canal near Craigmarloch and run close to it for several miles. The canal's most tranquil, rural length would be irretrievably ruined. It was 1997 before it was announced that the existing A80 would after all be upgraded, and the piped crossing of the canal replaced by a bridge.

In October 1994 British Waterways announced its intention to apply to the National Lottery Millennium Fund for a grant towards restoration of the Forth & Clyde and Union Canals: from sea to sea, and from Glasgow to Edinburgh. The Millennium Link, as the scheme was named, involves removal of some thirty-two obstructions to navigation, and construction of a boat lift similar to a ferris wheel to link the two canals at Falkirk. It is the largest project of its kind in which British Waterways has ever been involved.

The progress of the bid has been far from straightforward. A grant of £32 million was eventually announced by the Millennium Commission early in 1997, only to be followed by difficulties in subsequent negotiations for matching funding. These events are a past too recent to be considered objectively in detail here: but as I write, in the spring of 1998, much design work has been done and the Millennium Link is going ahead.

Selected Further Reading

BOWMAN, A I *Kirkintilloch Shipbuilding* Strathkelvin District Libraries & Museums, Bishopbriggs 1983.

BOWMAN, A I *Swifts and Queens* Strathkelvin District Libraries & Museums, Bishopbriggs 1984.

BOWMAN, A I *The Gipsy o' Kirky: SS Gipsy Queen* Strathkelvin District Libraries & Museums, Bishopbriggs 1987.

BROWN, H *Exploring the Edinburgh to Glasgow Canals* The Stationery Office Ltd, Edinburgh 1997.

CAMERON, A D *The Caledonian Canal* third edition Canongate Academic, Edinburgh 1994.

DUCKWORTH, C L D & Langmuir, G E *Clyde River and Other Steamers* third edition Brown Son & Ferguson Ltd, Glasgow 1972.

DUCKWORTH, C L D & Langmuir, G E *West Highland Steamers* third edition, T Stephenson & Sons Ltd, Prescot 1967.

GRAHAM, D *Sunset on the Clyde* Neil Wilson Publishing, Glasgow 1993.

HADFIELD, C *Thomas Telford's Temptation* M & M Baldwin, Cleobury Mortimer 1993.

HALDANE, A R B *New Ways through the Glens* third edition, House of Lochar, Colonsay 1995.

HANDLEY, J E *The Navvy in Scotland* Cork University Press, Cork 1970.

HUTTON, G *A Forth & Clyde Canalbum* Richard Stenlake, Ochiltree 1991.

HUTTON, G *Monkland: The Canal That Made Money* Richard Stenlake, Ochiltree 1993.

LINDSAY, J *The Canals of Scotland* David & Charles, Newton Abbot 1968.

McDONALD, D *The Clyde Puffer* third edition, House of Lochar, Colonsay 1996.

MARTIN, D *The Forth & Clyde Canal: A Kirkintilloch View* Strathkelvin District Libraries & Museums 1977.

MORRISON, I *Landscape with Lake Dwellings: The Crannogs of Scotland* Edinburgh University Press, Edinburgh 1985.

MOWAT, R J C *The Logboats of Scotland* Oxbow Books, Oxford 1996.

NEILL, J *Records and Reminiscences of Bonhill Parish* 1912, re-issued Hoddesden 1979.

OSBORNE, B D *The Ingenious Mr Bell* Argyll Publishing, Glendaruel 1995.

PATERSON, L *The Light in the Glens: The Rise and Fall of the Puffer Trade* House of Lochar, Colonsay 1996.

PRATT, E A *Scottish Canals and Waterways* Selwyn & Blount, London 1922.

THOMAS, J, revised Paterson, A J S *A Regional History of the Railways of Great Britain* vol VI *Scotland: The Lowlands and the Borders* David & Charles, Newton Abbot 1984.

Magazines

BW Monthly (British Waterways staff newspaper, available to the public on subscription)

Canal News (Forth & Clyde Canal Society)

LUCS News (Linlithgow Union Canal Society)

Paddle Wheels (Paddle Steamer Preservation Society)

Waterways World Burton-on-Trent monthly

Places to Visit

Museums and Visitor Centres:

Edinburgh: The Edinburgh Canal Centre, 27 Baird Road, Ratho, Midlothian EH28 8RA; 0131 333 1320/1251/1629: Bridge Inn & Visitor Centre beside the Union Canal at Ratho; restaurant boats, trip boats.

Edinburgh: Museum of Scotland, Chambers Street; 0131 225 7534: canal-related items on display include nineteenth-century model of Blackhill inclined plane.

Coatbridge: Summerlee Heritage Park, Heritage Way, Coatbridge, ML5 1QD; 01236 431261: includes restored length of Monkland Canal, canalside boatbuilding shop, full-size replica passage boat *Vulcan*.

Kenmore: The Scottish Crannog Centre, Croft-na-Caber, Kenmore, Loch Tay, Perthshire, PH15 2HW; 01887 830583: reconstruction of crannog of c500 BC and exhibition. Seasonal opening.

Kirkintilloch: Auld Kirk Museum; 0141 775 1185: includes small displays of photographs, models and artefacts relating to Forth & Clyde Canal and canalside shipbuilding.

Linlithgow: Linlithgow Union Canal Society, Canal Basin, Manse Road, Linlithgow, West Lothian EH49 6AJ; 01506 671215: canal museum, tearoom, trip boats, rowing boats and outboard boats for hire; weekends in summer season.

Trip boats, in addition to those mentioned above, include:

Forth & Clyde Canal: Forth & Clyde Canal Society trip boats from Kirkintilloch and Auchinstarry, summer weekends.

Loch Lomond: Sweeney's Cruises, Balloch (01389 752376);
MacFarlane & Son, Balmaha (01360 870214)(island mail boat);
and elsewhere: information from Tourist Information Centre, The Old Station, Balloch (01389 753533).

Loch Katrine: West of Scotland Water, Trossachs pier (01877 376316); ss *Sir Walter Scott*, seasonal.

Loch Awe: Dalriada Steam Packet Co Ltd, Loch Awe pier (01838 200440). seasonal.

Caledonian Canal: Jacobite Cruises, Tomnahurich Bridge, Glenurquhart Road, Inverness (01463 233999), seasonal.
Motor cruisers and sailing craft can be hired on the Caledonian Canal; information from British Waterways, Muirtown Wharf, Inverness IV3 5LS (01463 233140).

Useful Addresses

British Waterways (Scotland), Canal House, 1 Applecross Street, Glasgow, G4 9SP (0141 332 6936).

Loch Lomond Park Authority, The Old Station, Balloch Road, Balloch, Dunbartonshire, G83 8SS (01389 753311).

Dumfries & Galloway Council Ranger Service, 4 Market Street, Castle Douglas, DG7 1BE (01556 502351) (for Loch Ken).

Loch Lomond Steamship Company, Pier Road, Balloch, G83 8XQ (01389 711865) (for paddle steamer *Maid of the Loch*).

Addresses and telephone numbers for British Waterways departments and for many waterway societies appear in *Canalmanac* published annually by Waterways World Ltd, The Well House, High Street, Burton-on-Trent, Staffs DE14 1JQ.

Other titles from NMS Publishing

Scotland's Past in Action series

Fishing & Whaling

Sporting Scotland

Farming

Spinning & Weaving

Building Railways

Making Cars

Leaving Scotland

Feeding Scotland

Going to School

Going to Church

Scots in Sickness & Health

Going on Holiday

Going to Bed

Shipbuilding

Scottish Bicycles and Tricycles

Forthcoming titles: *Scottish Engineering: the machine makers, Getting Married in Scotland*

Scots Lives series

The Gentle Lochiel

Elsie Inglis

Miss Cranston

Mungo Park

Anthology series

Treasure Islands

Scotland's Weather

Scottish Endings

The Thistle at War

Archive photography series

Bairns

Into the Foreground

To See Oursels

Poetry Series

Present Poets
Scotland & the Sea
The Spirit of Flight

General

Robert Burns, Farmer
Tartan
Scenery of Scotland
Viking-age Gold & Silver of Scotland
The Scottish Home

Obtainable from all good bookshops or direct from:
NMS Publishing Limited,
Royal Museum,
Chambers Street,
Edinburgh EHI IJF.